CELEBRATION OF S[...]
Hampshi[...]

D. Fereday Glenn

IAN ALLAN
Publishing

First published 1994

ISBN 0 7110 2251 8

© David Fereday Glenn 1994

Published by Ian Allan Publishing

an imprint of Ian Allan Ltd, Terminal House,
Station Approach, Shepperton, Surrey TW17 8AS.
Printed by Ian Allan Printing Ltd, Coombelands
House, Coombelands Lane, Addlestone, Weybridge,
Surrey KT15 1HY.

Title page:
**Magic of steam: As the shadows lengthen, rebuilt 'West
Country' 4-6-2 No 34100** *Appledore* **makes an energetic
departure from the Down bay platform at Basingstoke with a
stopping train for Salisbury on 15 September 1966.**
D. A. Davies

Below:
**Almost at full tide and with the water as calm as a mill pond,
the stately crossing of Langstone viaduct by the 11.55am
branch train from Hayling to Havant created a mirror-image
of the octogenarian locomotive and two carriages on
7 January 1963. On this occasion the 'A1x' locomotive was
No 32661, a veteran of the Hayling service for many years
but which, sadly, was not secured for preservation.** *Author*

Front cover:
**With full stereo effect, Maunsell Class S15 4-6-0 No 30825
blasts beneath a footbridge to the west of Yeovil Town station as it comes off shed on 4 October 1962, ready for its
next spell of duty on the Southern main line.** *Author*

Back cover top:
**BR Standard 4-6-0 No 73001 leaves Broadstone with the
9am Bristol-Bournemouth Central service on 23 October
1965.** *Hugh Ballantyne*

Back cover bottom:
**The LCGB 'V2 Tour' from Waterloo to Weymouth via Yeovil is
seen on the Weymouth Quay line hauled by No 41298 on
3 July 1966.** *Hugh Ballantyne*

Contents

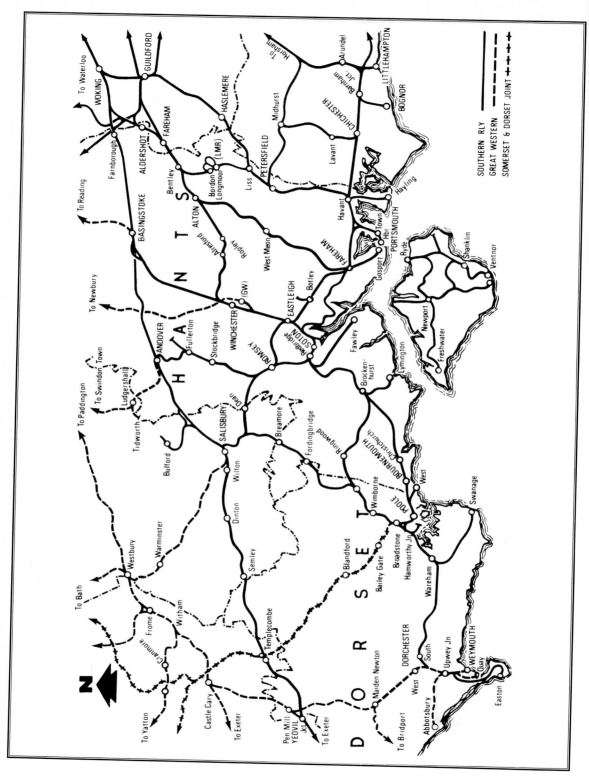

4

Introduction

Although the birth of the railway did not occur in either Hampshire or Dorset, the demise of the hissing, snorting monsters that formed the main motive power of trains for more than a century came last to this area (at least in the south). The main line from London to Basingstoke, Southampton, Bournemouth and Weymouth remained loyal to steam until 1967 — practically 20 years after the Nationalisation of the 'Big Four' and the inauguration of British Railways in 1948. With the benefit of hindsight, we can see that the decline of steam that followed the final flowering of new Standard designs in the 1950s was a kind of 'Golden Age'. Whatever the mistakes — political, managerial, financial — it was a time for steam such as will never come again. Now, as we approach not only the *fin de siècle* but also a new millennium, perhaps it is right we should celebrate the role of steam and the locomotives it begat. Steam, the engine of the Industrial Revolution, even

in its death-throes under the banner of British Railways still evoked a spirit of pride and admiration that has not been entirely quenched by the Computer Age.

It was with great pleasure that I accepted a commission to write one volume in a new series to mark a 'Celebration of Steam'. Even when I was still at school in the 1950s I used to submit occasional black-and-white pictures to Ian Allan for possible publication in either the regional 'ABCs' or *Trains Illustrated*, so my connection with this publisher goes back almost 40 years. When researching photographs recently for this book I came across

Typical of generations of Southern freight trains to or from Southampton, Class S15 4-6-0 No 30499 heads north through St Denys with the 1.22pm fitted vans from the Old (Eastern) Docks towards Feltham on 11 October 1960. Saved from the Barry scrapyard, this locomotive is a long-term restoration project on the Mid-Hants (Watercress Line) preserved railway. *John Courtney Haydon*

one or two of my early acceptances in a drawer at Shepperton. I also found some submitted by my old school friend, John Courtney Haydon, whose enlarger and primitive darkroom at Dibden Purlieu were responsible for processing my initial efforts; I am glad to be able to return the compliment now.

My own links with Hampshire and, to a lesser extent, Dorset go back a long way for I was born in Portsmouth and educated there and at Petersfield before becoming an Articled Clerk to a solicitor in the city of my birth. Then, towards the end of my training in the law, I spent some months with another firm of solicitors in Bournemouth — it was the summer of 1962, that fateful year when the wondrous Somerset & Dorset line suffered a grievous blow by having its summer through

services withdrawn for ever after September. The perennial problem with being an Articled Clerk was of being an unpaid student, a fact that caused no end of difficulty when funding one's hobby of watching and photographing trains. Both the cost of travel and of processing films ate into the modest budget, factors that bred economy of a kind that today's enthusiasts would scarcely appreciate! With large format 2¼in square negatives on 120 size film — only 12 to a roll — one was unable to afford the luxury of 'taking movie pictures with a still camera' such as many SLR practitioners take for granted these days. Rather, a single exposure had to serve, the result having to stand (or fall) thanks to a combination of favourable weather conditions and good fortune in more or less equal proportions. With the passage of time and the steady erosion of older steam locomotives, to say nothing of the closure of less economic

routes that tended to be their speciality, it became more and more difficult to maintain variety — so I turned increasingly to colour before it was too late. From the autumn of 1961 onwards I had access to a useful Kodak Retinette 35mm camera, that served to record the last years of steam power at work on British Railways together with the colourful Longmoor Military Railway before it was all gone. Perhaps about a thousand colour transparencies, all told, hold the key to the last six years of BR steam in the south, and it is this 'core' collection that invariably proves popular at club meetings or illustrated talks I have been invited to give. A handful have reached a wider audience by appearing on the jacket or dustcover of my various transport books.

Both Hampshire and Dorset are fortunate to have an example of a successful preserved standard gauge ex-British Railways line today, where those too young to remember the first two decades of BR steam can savour something of the atmosphere (though the engines were seldom as clean as they are today!). Those of us old enough to recall the 'first coming' can wallow in harmless nostalgia and recapture a measure of former delights. But the most exciting development of recent years has been the reappearance — albeit on a strictly limited basis — of steam-hauled trains on selected sections of the remaining BR network. A former S&D '7F' 2-8-0 has roused the echoes on the single track between Andover Junction and Ludgershall, rebuilt 'Merchant Navy' 4-6-2 *Clan Line* traversed the West of England route from Salisbury to Yeovil Junction (turning on the turntable there) while another Bulleid Pacific has brought the unmistakable sight and smell of steam to the Bournemouth main line on a nocturnal excursion from London (Waterloo). While this book may concern itself primarily with what I have termed the 'Golden Age' of BR steam traction, our celebration can encompass the incredible achievements not only of the erstwhile men of steam but also the dedicated groups of preservationists and the National Railway Museum, who have made it possible for this remarkable invention to continue towards a new millennium.

Vivat Vapor!

David Fereday Glenn
Catisfield, England
December 1993

East Hampshire and the Magnetism of Portsmouth Harbour

The earliest main line to be built with the intention of linking London with the Hampshire coast opened throughout between Nine Elms and Southampton in 1840, the same year as the Penny Post was introduced. But local pride in Portsmouth was offended until the railway changed its name to the London & South Western, nor was it entirely satisfied when a branch line from Bishopstoke (now Eastleigh) was extended through Botley and Fareham to Gosport in 1841. The populace of Portsmouth was mollified when the London, Brighton & South Coast Railway constructed a route west of Chichester, piercing the Hilsea Lines' fortifications in 1847, promptly followed by the LSWR building a spur from Fareham through Cosham to Portcreek Junction the following year. The tracks south of Portcreek Junction became the joint property of both railways thereafter until their amalgamation into the Southern Railway in 1923.

It was not long before Portsmuthians were again complaining about the long-winded journey — by either LSWR or LBSCR — to London. It was left to an independent contractor, Thomas Brassey, to survey a route south from Guildford to meet the LBSCR's tracks at Havant; the Portsmouth Direct line had to be built far more sparingly than the Basingstoke-Southampton route, conforming to the undulating nature of the landscape rather than carving a way straight through. It was this awkward terrain that made the

Opposite page:
On 9 May 1962, some 120 years after the opening of Hampshire's first branch line, Class N 2-6-0 No 31413 shunts across Spring Garden Lane, Gosport, with a freight for RN Clarence Yard. This single track extension beyond Gosport station led to the platform formerly used by Queen Victoria during her visits to Osborne on the Isle of Wight, and involved building a short tunnel beneath the ramparts of the old fortifications. *All uncredited photographs by the Author*

Below:
On Saturdays only in summer a separate through train ran from Plymouth to Portsmouth in addition to the main service to Brighton. This 1960s picture has captured air-smoothed 'Battle of Britain' light Pacific No 34075 *264 Squadron* with the 10.20am from Plymouth shortly after restarting from Cosham, approaching Cosham Junction signalbox before taking the curve to Portcreek Junction.
S. Creer

Portsmouth Direct a difficult line to operate both with steam and, since 1937, electric traction, since it suffers from extremes of weather and is particularly prone to disruption from leaves on the track in late autumn. For all that, it offers a wonderful panorama for the passing passenger in all its seasons during daylight hours.

While the terminal at Portsmouth was a splendidly imposing structure situated in the central part of town, it did not serve the needs of ferry passengers to either Gosport or the Isle of Wight who were obliged to take a horse-cab or, after 1865, a horse-drawn tram to the Pier. The extension of urban tramways in the 1870s led the two rival railways to build a high-level route over a busy thoroughfare and thence on an embankment to a new interchange with the ferries and harbour launches outside the Dockyard in 1876. Apart from the closure of several minor branches into naval or military establishments, plus the shortlived Southsea Railway from Fratton, the railway lines serving Portsmouth have remained virtually unaltered for more than a century.

The same cannot be said for the various branch railways that were constructed to link rural communities to one of the main lines. The LSWR branch from Petersfield to Midhurst opened in 1864 but suffered total closure even before the Beeching era. Further south, an independent line serving Hayling Island (worked by the LBSCR) came into full use in 1867, crossing from the mainland on an impressive timber viaduct complete with swing bridge for local shipping. Although busy in summer with holidaymakers, who could save hours by using the train compared with the congested narrow roads, closure was imposed in November 1963 thus bringing to an end the last passenger duties performed by William Stroudley's famous 'Terrier' 0-6-0Ts; the class had been introduced to Hayling in the 1890s. Hampshire's very first branch line, to Gosport, remained open for freight until 1969 although passenger traffic had been withdrawn in 1953. More minor branches, to Stokes Bay and Lee-on-the-Solent, ceased long ago. Another 'twig', opened in the same year as that to Stokes Bay (1863), survived rather longer as a purely freight facility; the grandiose plans for a branch northeastward from Botley towards Petersfield never progressed beyond Bishop's Waltham. Passenger traffic ceased at the end of 1932, but goods trains ran until April 1962.

One more branch came into existence more in hope than anticipation in 1903, linking Alton with Fareham via the Meon Valley. After 1849 when a line had been put into place between Guildford and Farnham, then extended to Alton three years later, it was only a matter of time before local interests saw the need to press on to Winchester (the Mid-Hants route of 1865). With a Light Railway from Basingstoke to Alton up and running by 1901, the Meon Valley was the last great open space in this area not connected to the LSWR or one of its satellites. The danger from the LSWR viewpoint was that its arch rival, the Great Western, might be tempted to strike through the gap to fulfil a perceived ambition to reach the coast — this may not have been so far-fetched, in fact, since the GWR *did* gain access to Southampton via both the Didcot, Newbury & Southampton and the Midland & South Western Junction Railway after the Grouping. In the event, the Meon Valley line remained a quiet backwater throughout its existence, ceasing to function as a complete entity in 1955; the lower section between Knowle Junction and Droxford remained open for goods for a further seven years, while the northern extremity from Butts Junction (Alton) to Farringdon survived a little longer in a similar capacity.

Midway between Alton and Farnham, right on the Hampshire/Surrey border, a short branch was established in 1905 from Bentley to the army garrison town of Bordon. Soon afterwards construction began of the Woolmer Instructional Military Railway from Bordon to Longmoor camp, intended for training Royal Engineers in the building and operation of railways at home or abroad in time of war. The system was gradually extended until it linked up with the Portsmouth Direct line at Liss Junction in the 1930s. As the threat of war again cast its shadow over Europe, the Longmoor Military Railway (as it had been renamed) assumed much greater significance and, following the outbreak of hostilities in 1939, the system was rapidly expanded to a total of 71 miles of trackwork including the six-mile Hollywater loop. Because the military authorities had insufficient locomotives of their own, additional engines were hired from the four main railways — GWR, LMS, LNER and SR — to meet these exceptional needs. In preparation for the time when it would become necessary to take the battle across the Channel, the Ministry of Supply designed and built a small number of 'standard' types, testing and storing them on the Longmoor system and elsewhere in anticipation of D-Day. With the USA as an ally against the Axis powers, two similar 'off the shelf' designs were shipped across from North America to help the war effort and these also appeared at Longmoor. With D-Day finally set for 6 June 1944, the various 'Austerity' locomotives were moved to their embarkation points and most served on the continent before disposal. A few were retained by the military, one of the most famous being No 600 *Gordon* , a WD 2-10-0 that stayed at Longmoor until the LMR was closed down at the end of 1969; it is now preserved in working order on the Severn Valley Railway together with an LMS-designed '8F' 2-8-0 (No 8233, BR No 48773) that saw service in Egypt before joining BR's stock in 1957.

In this area of Hampshire the main steam locomotive depots were at Eastleigh (71A), Basingstoke (70D) and Fratton (71D, later recoded 70F). In addition, Guildford (70C) and Salisbury (72B) provided the motive power for some routes or services, while engines from further afield might appear on specific duties that brought them to a particular destination or passing through. An instance of such through working was of Brighton (75A) locomotives on services to Bournemouth, Cardiff or Plymouth; in each case they headed trains along the electrified coastal route through Worthing and Chichester to Havant, before avoiding Portsmouth on the triangle and continuing via Cosham, Fareham and Netley to Southampton. While such services soon

became the preserve of Bulleid Pacifics of the lighter 'West Country' and 'Battle of Britain' classes, some notable visitors included Marsh Atlantics of Class H2, three-cylinder 2-6-0s of Class U1, ex-SECR 'L' class 4-4-0s and '4MT' 2-6-4Ts of both LMS and BR Standard designs. For the tank engines, in particular, journeys between Brighton and Bournemouth or Salisbury (where locomotives were changed) must have been among the longest to be undertaken in postwar years. Very rarely, for example if the Basingstoke-Southampton route was blocked (as happened occasionally in the build-up to electrification), certain services might be diverted. The Portsmouth Direct route was the most likely to be chosen, unless the track occupation was north of Winchester, in which case services could run via Alton and the Mid-Hants line 'over the Alps'. Exceptionally, on a couple of Sundays in November 1964, Waterloo-Bournemouth trains ran from Eastleigh to Fareham (where they reversed and changed engines) before continuing via Netley to Southampton. These diversions were all the more spectacular since they included the 'Bournemouth Belle' Pullman service; this train ceased with electrification in July 1967, despite being diesel-hauled for much of the last few months of its existence.

Below:
Both the curvature of the track and the rural nature of the Portsmouth Direct line can be glimpsed in this study of Bulleid 4-6-2 No 34086 *219 Squadron*, working hard 'against the collar' with a heavy Ocean Liner Express from Southampton Docks to Waterloo. Diverted because of engineering works on 27 June 1965, the engine was faced with an uphill struggle north of Petersfield as far as Haslemere.
R. H. Tunstall

Above:

Until closure in February 1955, the most regular steam-hauled passenger train to be found at Petersfield (on the Portsmouth Direct line) was the branch service to Midhurst. Comprising one or two push-pull carriages of pre-Grouping origin and usually in the care of an appropriately equipped 0-4-4T, the Midhurst train had its own bay platform on the opposite side of the level crossing from the main station. In this early morning vista from the footbridge an ex-LSWR Class M7 0-4-4T and corridor push-pull set No 737 wait hopefully for custom in the bay beside the dairy — note the traditional milk churns on the platform. *E. C. Griffith; Author's Collection*

Left:

Weekday goods traffic between Petersfield and Midhurst was catered for by a single train in each direction. Until the closure of the Midhurst-Cocking section of the branch to Chichester, following a culvert wash-out in November 1951, the goods was operated by a Guildford (70C) engine from the Petersfield end, but thereafter it brought a Horsham (75D) or Three Bridges (75E) loco to Petersfield before returning eastward at 1.35pm. All four examples of the ex-LBSCR Class E5x 0-6-2Ts appeared on the goods at various times, with Nos 32570 and 32576 providing the motive power for the special 'Hampshireman' excursion that ran over the branch on Sunday, 6 February 1955 (the day after it closed to all traffic). Coupled bunker to bunker, these two veterans are seen at Rogate station on their way back light to Horsham shed, the last BR engines to travel over the line from Petersfield. *R. C. Riley*

Above:
Galloping along with a lightweight Christmas parcels train, Standard 4 2-6-0 No 76031 passes Froyle between Bentley and Alton as storm clouds gather during the afternoon of 12 December 1966. This was the final festive season for steam haulage of these mail trains — note the odd mixture of stock. *E. C. Griffith*

Below:
A Maunsell corridor set (No 245) was rather more comfortable fare than the ageing push-pull units generally provided for Mid-Hants passengers. Class M7 No 30479 was the motive power on the evening of 20 June 1952, preparing to leave Alton for Winchester City and Southampton. *G. H. Robin*

Above:
The immaculate condition of LMR steam engines in their final years contrasted starkly with their counterparts on BR. On 10 January 1966 No 102 paused at Oakhanger with a brake van from Bordon, the connecting BR goods from Farnham to Bordon (BR) having been cancelled that day. This engine was not equipped with vacuum brake and was thus unable to work passenger services. Built by Hunslet in 1943 as No 75035 and named *Caen* at some stage, it worked at Longmoor from 1959 until sold for scrap in August 1967.

Below:
Resplendent with red lining, Hunslet 0-6-0ST No 195 sets out from Longmoor Downs early on the morning of 30 June 1967 with ex-BR non-corridor brake 2nd coach No AD3031 in tow, to form the first passenger train of the day from Liss Junction. This was the last year in which steam power was regularly employed at the LMR.

Above:
Having built up a good head of steam during the initial run from Longmoor Downs, No 195 was preparing to run round its one-coach train while civilian employees boarded at Liss Junction on 30 June 1967. Built by Hunslet in 1953, this was the final season of activity on the LMR for this particular engine.

Below:
It had become customary to have one public Open Day at Longmoor each year (as a PR exercise, rather like Navy Days at Portsmouth), but with the demise of steam on BR plus the temporary lodging of privately-preserved locomotives on LMR tracks it was not difficult to justify an additional visiting day. On 21 September 1968 both 2-10-0 *Gordon* and 0-6-0ST *Errol Lonsdale* were in steam providing rides between Liss and Longmoor Downs. At the end of the day, No 600 *Gordon* is seen after arrival at Longmoor surrounded by admirers; built by the North British Co in Glasgow in 1943, it originally carried War Department number 73651.

Above:
On a cold, bright winter's day the diminutive Stroudley 0-6-0T No 32650 of Class A1x had steam to spare as it bustled out of the bay platform at Havant with the 11.35am service to Hayling Island on 26 January 1961. Note the spark arrestor attached to the elegant tapering LBSCR chimney.

Below:
On a cloudy Sunday morning, the 'spare' set of coaches was brought up from Fratton by a brace of 'Terrier' 0-6-0Ts. After waiting for the 10.5am service to Hayling to vacate the bay, Class A1x tanks Nos 32646 (leading) and 32650 double-head the stock across the complex of electrified tracks to reach the safety of the branch on 22 July 1962. Double-heading of services on the Hayling line itself was extremely rare, but in summer the provision of two engines to bring the second set of carriages on Saturdays and Sundays was commonplace.

Above:

It is comparatively rare that the southern counties receive more than a sprinkling of snow, but the winter of 1962/63 was a notable exception. On 28 December 1962 the snowfall was fresh: Class A1x 0-6-0T No 32678, wreathed in steam, had charge of the 11.35am Havant-Hayling Island service. After a brief pause at Langston, the little engine cautiously restarted from the simple platform on its southbound journey.

Below:

On summer Saturdays and Sundays a half-hourly interval service was provided in each direction between Havant and Hayling for much of the day. Alternate trains ran non-stop leaving one per hour to call at the intermediate points of Langston and North Hayling. On Sunday, 22 July 1962 Class A1x No 32650 skirts the wind-swept shoreline past North Hayling Halt with the 11.5am non-stop train to Hayling Island.

Left:
A number of Stroudley's 'Terriers' spent some years in the Isle of Wight, where they benefited from the enlargement of the coal bunkers. One of the 'A1x' class that remained throughout its long life on the mainland was No 32661, thus retaining its original small bunker (plus added coal rails) and toolbox. On 4 March 1960 this veteran was being coaled by hand at Hayling terminus, in preparation for working the 2.53pm 'mixed' back to Havant — two coaches stand in the main platform and a spare has been left in the bay on the right, while the goods yard is full of wagons.

Left:
Normal public trains over the Hayling branch ceased with the final service on Saturday, 2 November 1963. A last opportunity for enthusiasts from London to travel over the single line was arranged for Sunday, 3 November, with the oldest two 'Terriers' — one at either end of a five-coach rake — to power the train. Beautifully prepared for its swansong, Class A1x 0-6-0T No 32670 gleamed in the sunshine in the bay platform at Havant to await the special from London; it is now preserved on the Kent & East Sussex with two other examples of this famous design.

Left:
For a few weeks during the summer peak, special through services operated between the Midlands and the South Coast for the benefit of holidaymakers. One such service to run on Saturdays only was the 1.11pm from Portsmouth Harbour to Birmingham (Moor Street). On 13 July 1957 the train was powered by Western Region 4-6-0 No 4965 *Rood Ashton Hall*, seen awaiting departure from the curving Harbour platform alongside 4-COR 'Nelson' unit No 3125 on a routine fast electric service to London (Waterloo). *M. J. Foster*

Above:
By the 1960s, increasing use was being made of BR Standard 4-6-0s on inter-Regional trains. On 10 August 1963 Class 5 No 73114 *Etarre* was in charge of the 9.11am from Portsmouth Harbour to Wolverhampton (Low Level) at platform 3, with the RN semaphore tower of HM Dockyard beyond. *S. Creer*

Right:
Portsmouth Harbour station was visited by a special train during the afternoon of 24 February 1957. Though expected to arrive behind the last Marsh Atlantic, No 32424, in fact it was hauled by newly-built Standard 4 2-6-4T No 80152. To round off the day's proceedings, 'Schools' class 4-4-0 No 30929 *Malvern* (with double-chimney and painted in Brunswick-green livery) backed on to treat the passengers to a fast run to London via the Portsmouth Direct route. This picture shows *Malvern* easing past a 12-coach train of 'Nelson' EMUs, of which No 3131 was nearest the camera.

Above:
After World War 2 the sole rail access to Portsmouth Dockyard was via the short branch from Portsmouth & Southsea (High Level) to Unicorn Gate. The junction occurred part-way along platform 6, requiring Dockyard-bound trains to surmount the ramp to the High Level 'wrong line'. On 14 February 1956 push-pull fitted Class O2 0-4-4T No 30207 roared past the end of platform 5 of the Low Level station in a determined effort to climb the adverse 1 in 61 gradient with the 1.57pm Fratton-Dockyard goods without stalling.

Below right:
The Low Level at Portsmouth & Southsea station comprised five platforms together with additional sidings for empty stock (steam and electric) and a turntable for smaller loco-motives. On 8 April 1957 the 2.33pm to Bristol (Temple Meads) was waiting to depart from the longest of the Low Level platforms (No 5), with Class U 2-6-0 No 31792 at the head of WR stock. Booked to run non-stop to Southampton after picking up at Fratton, this service was one of the very few not to call at Fareham *en route.*

Right:
The 1.57pm Fratton-Portsmouth Dockyard goods descends the steep gradient from High Level station to cross Edinburgh Road level crossing on 20 April 1956. Ex-LBSCR Class E1 0-6-0T No 32694 is in charge on this occasion, as the train sweeps round the sharp curve past Victoria Park, behind the Stanhope Road offices of Portsmouth & Sunderland Newspapers.

Right:
Alongside the roundhouse at Fratton on 27 November 1959 stood one of the Class H15 4-6-0s No 30474. This was a very mixed class, which included rebuilt Drummond locomotives as well as the Urie pattern along with 10 locomotives built after the Grouping — 26 in total. With 6ft 0in driving wheels, the class was useful for mixed traffic work and could be substituted for the more glamorous 'King Arthurs' if need be. This example was withdrawn in 1960.

Left:
Christmas operations sometimes provided some unusual workings: even so, Fratton (70F) witnessed some strange bedfellows in 1960. On 22 December the solitary ex-SECR Class D1 4-4-0 to have been transferred to Eastleigh, No 31735, was rostered to work the lunchtime parcels and ECS train from Fratton yard, loaded to 335 tons. The Maunsell rebuild struggled to get the heavy train moving, while alongside stood a freshly-overhauled ex-WR 0-6-0PT (No 4689 of Weymouth) on loan for shunting and local trip duties.

Left:
Though designed by Bulleid as a heavy freight locomotive to assist in the war effort, the curious 'Q1' Austerity 0-6-0s were sometimes pressed into service on passenger traffic. On 6 January 1960 No 33010 leaned to the curve as it passed Fratton non-stop with the 12.15pm Portsmouth & Southsea-Plymouth stock, which it worked as far as Fareham for attachment to the main train from Brighton. Doyen of the class, No 33001 (now with its original Southern number C1) has been preserved and restored to active use on the Bluebell line in East Sussex.

Above:
Several times each weekday a goods train ran between Fratton yard and Portsmouth naval dockyard. On 22 October 1959 an ex-LBSCR Class E1 0-6-0T, designed by Stroudley, was employed on the job: No 32694 puffed sedately beneath the ornate footbridge at Fratton station with the 1.57pm for Unicorn Gate. Note the lack of any headcode disc or lamp!

Below:
One of the Urie-designed Class S15 4-6-0s, No 30504, makes a spirited exit from Portsmouth & Southsea (Low Level) station with the 12.15pm through coaches for Plymouth on 14 April 1960. Still in 'Blood and Custard' livery, the four-coach set (No 888) is to be attached to the rear of the Brighton-Plymouth service at Fareham.

Above:
After being slowed to walking pace, a Bristol-Portsmouth through train is shown the green flag at the approach to Cosham by the hand signalman. The train of WR carriages is hauled by a Drummond Class T9 4-4-0 (No 30725 of Salisbury shed), which appears impatient to be off after the delay.

This interesting picture shows the Up and Down sidings that formerly straddled the Fareham-Portsmouth line just to the west of Cosham station; also some of the elderly ex-LSWR non-corridor stock used on local services until 1957. Together with the 'pre-fab' bungalows by the lineside, the whole scene has a fine period flavour and dates from c1950.
The News, Portsmouth

Right:

The temporary non-availability of Salisbury turntable in March 1960 meant that the usual engine-changing facility there was suspended. Through services between Portsmouth, Bristol and Cardiff had to be worked throughout by the same locomotive and, due to restrictions over the viaduct at Bursledon, these were mostly in the hands of 2-6-0s of both Southern and Great Western origins. On 24 March the 9.33am from Portsmouth & Southsea to Cardiff General was powered by Churchward-designed Mogul No 6338 exhibiting reporting number '264', spotted climbing away from Cosham past the allotments in fine style.

Right:

The mixed-traffic 'Hall' class 4-6-0 was a regular visitor to the Portsmouth area until 1961, when WR DMUs took over the services to and from Reading. On 11 June 1952 No 4939 *Littleton Hall* headed the 2.45pm Portsmouth & Southsea-Reading General train formed of a three-coach Bulleid set plus van, recorded in the cutting between Portchester and Fareham while still accelerating from the last station stop.
S. F. Clark

Right:

An unexpected cold snap on New Year's Eve caught the Southern Region napping — on 1 January 1962 a number of services were disrupted or delayed by the overnight snow. Veteran Drummond 'Black Motor' 0-6-0 No 30306 was turned out for the 7.50am Eastleigh-Gosport goods and was busy shunting by Fareham West signalbox rather later than the scheduled departure time of 10.10am when captured by the camera.

Left:
Hampshire DMUs took over regular operation of local services between Portsmouth, Southampton, Eastleigh and Salisbury with the commencement of the winter timetable for 1957. However, steam remained in charge of the Andover trains for a few weeks longer and, on 19 October 1957, 'Greyhound' 'T9' 4-4-0 No 30117 lifted the 2.57pm Portsmouth & Southsea-Andover Junction out of Fareham via the double-track avoiding lines towards Eastleigh.

Left:
Heading the Cardiff-Brighton through train on 1 September 1955, Standard Class 4 2-6-4T No 80019 portrays one of the long cross-country journeys undertaken by engines of this type based at 75A. No 80019 was built at Brighton Works in October 1951 and allocated initially to Tunbridge Wells before returning to Brighton. The Standards displaced similar Class 4MT tanks built at Brighton to LMS design, which had also been tried out on this sort of task in the early 1950s; the engine is pictured at Fareham beside the original (1841) part of the station building, before shedding a part of the train for Portsmouth.

Left:
After the demise of the small class of ex-LBSCR freight engines (Class C3) in the early 1950s, their place was taken by the more successful rebuilds of Class C2. A number of the 'C2x' variants featured a double-domed boiler, a characteristic that was shared with the 'E5x' and 'E6x' 0-6-2T classes since the boilers were often exchanged during visits to the works. During a spell when it was equipped with one of these double-domed boilers, 'Vulcan' 0-6-0 No 32549 backed on to the Portsmouth carriages of a through train from Plymouth at Fareham during the afternoon of 29 April 1955.

Above:
The historic terminus at Gosport was denied a passenger service after June 1953, but continued to see regular freight traffic long afterwards. Typical of day-to-day activities in the early 1960s was the appearance of Class U 2-6-0 No 31808 with the 2.15pm goods for Fareham and Eastleigh. Note the metal overall roof that was installed as a replacement for the original timber structure bombed during World War 2.

Below:
As the shadows begin to lengthen, Class Q1 0-6-0 No 33037 gives tongue starting the 6.29pm freight from Fareham to Eastleigh past Fareham West box on 27 July 1961; the train originated as the 4.20pm from Havant, hence the three-disc headcode. This working incorporated wagons off the 5.35pm from Gosport. The engine from the latter train then travelled light back to Eastleigh.

The fore-and-aft motion of an 0-6-0 tender engine (primarily intended for freight haulage at relatively low speeds) had to be experienced to be believed when working passenger trains. In the best tradition of these brief 'flings', Class Q No 30542 powers its four Mark 1 carriages through the cutting between Fareham and Portchester with the Portsmouth portion of the Cardiff-Brighton service on 9 April 1960.

Temporarily hijacked for passenger duty because of the snow, Class K 2-6-0 No 32343 of Brighton (75A) pulled the four-coach set forming the Portsmouth-Cardiff General portion clear of platform 3 at Fareham on 1 January 1962. While waiting for the arrival of the main train from Brighton set No 888 stood nearby on the Gosport branch; in due course it was to be attached to the rear before the combined stock set off for Southampton and Salisbury behind a rebuilt Bulleid Light Pacific. The ex-LBSCR Mogul had brought the green Mark 1s up from Portsmouth Harbour tender-first, no mean achievement for the crew in the arctic conditions prevailing!

Right:
On weekdays one of the heaviest trains regularly using the double-track route from Fareham avoiding the Funtley tunnel was the ECS duty leaving Fratton yard at 11.8am. On 15 March 1958 one of the 'King Arthur' class of 4-6-0s, No 30457 *Sir Bedivere*, plodded purposefully past the electricity sub-station to the north of Fareham station on its way to Eastleigh. Though built under Maunsell's direction, the 10 Class N15s, Nos 30448-57, retained the Urie pattern of cab roof and were known as 'Eastleigh Arthurs'; most were based at Salisbury and handled a lot of passenger traffic over the West of England main line to Yeovil and Exeter.

Right:
One of the 'Mickey Mouse' Class 2MT 2-6-2Ts allocated to Eastleigh (71A) regularly alternated with a Drummond 'M7' on the 3.45pm local train from Portsmouth & Southsea to Romsey during the final summer of steam operation. On 18 May 1957 No 41293 was making a spirited ascent of the 1 in 100 on the double track from Fareham towards Knowle Junction with a vintage set of three ex-LSWR non-corridor coaches in tow, just below Highlands Road bridge. Today no trains run here, and gardens have encroached upon the former trackbed where Eastleigh-bound traffic once did battle with the adverse gradient.

Above:
On summer Saturdays Fareham enjoyed a wide variety of visiting locomotives passing through on holiday trains. On 24 May 1958 the 3.28pm from Portsmouth Harbour to Wolverhampton (Low Level) produced green-liveried 4-6-0 No 7911 *Lady Margaret Hall* hauling a rake of traditional ex-GWR Collett coaches in the colourful 'Blood and Custard' paintwork of the early BR period. With Class 'A' headlamps in position ready for the transition to WR metals at Reading, the train is pictured passing Highlands Road bridge on the 1 in 100 gradient towards Eastleigh. Today the trackbed is popular with walkers in the direction of Knowle Junction.

Below:
Beyond Knowle Junction towards Eastleigh there is a single, short tunnel at Tapnage. Generally, the morning Reading-Portsmouth train was powered by a WR 4-6-0, but on 23 April 1960 a three cylinder 'Schools' 4-4-0 (No 30918 *Hurstpierpoint*) burst from the southern portal at the head of Bulleid set No 791. It can only be assumed that a shortage of motive power at Reading WR depot (81D) or a last-minute failure caused the Class V engine to be substituted from the SR shed (70E); 'Schools' locomotives were frequently found on Reading-Redhill services at the time.

Above:
Rather like Fairford in Gloucestershire, Bishop's Waltham was designed as a through station, with the goods yard beyond (beside what would have been an extension to somewhere else!). However, it was not to be, and after reduction of status to goods only the branch lingered on until the Beeching era. Shortly before closure to all traffic, Class 2MT 2-6-2T No 41214 was found shunting beside the distinctive goods shed at Bishop's Waltham in preparation for working the 11.10am back to Botley; the date was 1 March 1962.

Below:
For most of its length the Bishop's Waltham branch ran through very rural country away from public access, but at one point it came within yards of the B3035 road for a short distance. On Sunday, 22 May 1960 an engineers' train was attending to the ballast close by culvert 5A with Standard Class 4MT 2-6-0 No 76059 working tender-first. The use of a tender engine for any purpose was a rarity on this rural backwater — the author has seen no other photographic evidence of it occurring on the Bishop's Waltham branch.

Left:

Still giving good service more than 40 years after its introduction into traffic on the LSWR by Robert Urie, Class S15 No 30511 steams majestically out of Funtley tunnel on the original 1841 route to Fareham (and Gosport) with the 11.47am Salisbury-Chichester goods on 22 February 1963. Most of the 20 members of the 'S15' class, designed by Urie, were withdrawn in 1963 — just two survive, both on the Mid-Hants Railway.

Above:

As dieselisation was extended, steam was left with long-distance passenger trains and most of the freight. In April 1964 a rather shabby 4-6-0, one of the later Maunsell Class S15s, drifted past Knowle Halt with the 11.47am Salisbury-Chichester goods. No 30838 was passing the private siding for Knowle Hospital which, unusually by this time, had a van in residence. The brick goods shed, no doubt built with the products of the local brickworks at Funtley, still stands today, though adapted for light industrial use.

Right:

After calling briefly at Knowle Halt, Standard Class 4MT 2-6-0 No 76059 was still accelerating briskly as it passed the disused siding at Funtley brickworks on the single track to Fareham. The Mogul was working the 9.10am Reading General-Portsmouth & Southsea service on 26 March 1960.

Left:
Engines newly overhauled at Eastleigh Works were sometimes run-in on freight duties before being despatched to their 'home' shed. For example, on 21 March 1962, Standard Class 4MT 2-6-4T No 80151 was discovered shunting the branch goods at Wickham, retrieving a flat wagon from the end-loading dock before continuing to Droxford. The Meon Valley line lost its passenger service in February 1955. Now there is a modern housing estate on the site of Wickham station with few reminders that a railway had once linked Fareham with Alton.

Left:
In the autumn of its days as part of the BR network — and then only for freight traffic — Wickham station played host to the 12.20pm Fareham-Droxford goods on 4 October 1961. Class U 2-6-0 No 31808, one of the Moguls to have been rebuilt from the ill-fated 'River' tanks of the SECR, was standing in the former Up platform before shunting the yard; the loop through the Down platform had been removed early in 1957.

Left:
The final 'official' BR train ran on Friday, 27 April 1962 over the southern stump of the Meon Valley line. Powered as usual by a Mogul running tender-first to Droxford, Class U No 31618 had some enthusiasts on board the two brake vans as it pulled out of Wickham station. Happily, this engine was not scrapped and now performs on the Bluebell Railway on both passenger and (demonstration) goods trains.

Main Line to Southampton, with Adjoining Branches

The Southern's historic main line between London — originally Nine Elms, later extended to Waterloo — and Southampton was completed in 1840. West of Woking and Pirbright Junction the route is four-track today as far as Worting Junction, reflecting how busy the north Hampshire corridor through Farnborough and Basingstoke has become. Even now, a century and a half after it was built, there is a sense of grandeur about the massive way in which the London & Southampton Railway conceived its purpose: for mile after mile the tracks are straight and, after bearing more southerly beyond Basingstoke, a string of tunnels and deep cuttings bears witness to the company's determination not to be deflected from its task.

At the approach to Winchester a branch from Alton and Alresford — the Mid-Hants route — formerly came in from the east. Opened in 1865, it was an early candidate for dieselisation in 1957 although local freight traffic and periodic diversions (when the main line was closed) remained the province of steam. Inexplicably, in view of its usefulness and traffic potential, the 17 miles between Alton and Winchester Junction were not included in the electrification programme (Alton had been electrified before World War 2) and the route was closed in the post-Beeching period. The 10 miles west of Alton as far as Alresford are now operational again under private ownership using both steam and diesel traction.

Close to the site of Winchester Junction, the main line crossed over another railway which once had ambitions for through traffic to Southampton. The Didcot, Newbury & Southampton Railway got as far south as its own station at Winchester (Chesil) by 1885, but then stalled until agreement with the LSWR could be reached for a link at Shawford Junction in 1891. Although the route was upgraded during World War 2, and provided a useful cross-country alternative for heavy freight traffic such as bulk oil trains, passenger services were withdrawn in

Below:
As late as 1966 the traditional 'puff and dart' lower-quadrant semaphore signals remained in use on the main line between Farnborough and Basingstoke. On 10 September that year 'Merchant Navy' 4-6-2 No 35023, bereft of nameplates, thundered through Fleet with an afternoon express from Bournemouth to Waterloo while the third-rail electrification spread further west. *A. D. McIntyre*

1960. From 1964 all but the southern stub between Bar End yard (Winchester) and Shawford Junction was closed, with total abandonment following in 1966. The DN&S line was responsible for the appearance on shed at Eastleigh during the 1950s and 1960s of ex-GWR 0-6-0s and 2-6-0s; in its last years as a through route for freight 71A played host to a succession of 2-8-0s (WD/Stanier '8F' as well as the Churchward '28xx' type) and Standard Class 9F 2-10-0s. Occasional visits were recorded by more exotic engines also, including ex-LMS 'Royal Scot' and 'Jubilee' 4-6-0s.

Left:
On the Hampshire/Surrey border east of Farnborough a rebuilt 'West Country' Pacific No 34044 (formerly *Woolacombe*) clatters through the deep wooded cutting with a Basingstoke-Waterloo stopping train on 15 April 1967. As is now well-known, the timeless lure of steam at speed on the main line has managed to transcend temporary banishment and expedience; since October 1971 it has made a progressive return to many parts of the BR network, albeit in a cameo role... *John R. P. Hunt*

Below:
Framed by a majestic five-arch bridge over the four-track main line on the Hampshire/Surrey border at milepost 31, rebuilt 'West Country' Pacific No 34001 (formerly *Exeter*) powers past with the all-Pullman 'Bournemouth Belle' on 30 April 1966. *J. L. McIvor*

On the outskirts of Southampton is St Denys Junction, where one of the more impressive station buildings has been refurbished in recent years to secure its future. The junction came into being with the opening of a branch to Netley in 1866, ostensibly to provide a rail link to the military hospital; 23 years later an extension was constructed through Bursledon and Swanwick to Fareham, thus linking Portsmouth and Southampton directly for the first time. A short branch was also laid from Netley station yard into the grounds of the hospital in 1900, but by the 1950s its use was sporadic and the line closed in 1955. From this period the railway steadily lost freight to road hauliers and brickworks sidings were taken out of use near Bursledon and at Funtley. The Shell oil sidings at Hamble survived the withdrawal of steam but closed in the 1980s.

The original terminal of the London & Southampton Railway still survives, but its platforms are gone and the station building has had other uses since closure in September 1966. Likewise, Ocean Village has arisen where once stood the Princess Alexandra Dock, beyond Canute Road, with all its maze of quays and sidings. The only street tramway

in Southampton to outlive the steam age was from Northam to Dibles Wharf, serving Corrall's fuel depot. At one time there had been as many as three such tramways serving the Itchen quays, but while Dibles Wharf continued to use steam engines — one a former BR 0-4-0T — into the 1970s, that track has since been lifted. Perhaps the saddest loss has been the Eastern Docks Ocean Terminal, where generations of boat trains waited upon the great liners: the distinctive building has been demolished and the sole surviving track across Canute Road lies rusty and disused. It is a different story, however, in the Western Docks — much of which was reclaimed from the sea in the 1930s. While appearances by visiting liners have diminished from their heyday, container freight traffic has given new life to sidings in the Millbrook area where Freightliners serve the terminal regularly.

Redbridge Sleeper Depot, beside the Test estuary, provided a haven for one of Drummond's little 0-4-0Ts of the 'C14' class for many years. Of the three examples that remained at Nationalisation, two normally shunted the Town Quay and adjoining Platform Road sidings — all that remained of a street tramway from the Terminus station beside Canute Road — and the third pottered around the sprawling Sleeper Depot. It had its own brick-built engine shed and the usual incumbent was No 77s, numbered into the Departmental series long before Nationalisation but previously LSWR No 745 (SR No 0745). When its two sisters, Nos 30588/9, were summoned for scrap in the mid-1950s, No 77s was 'borrowed' to deputise at the Town Quay until it, in turn, was withdrawn early in 1959. In its stead an Adams 'O2' 0-4-4T went to Redbridge until, in the fullness of time, it too was replaced by a 'USA' 0-6-0T up to the end of steam.

Left:
A fine portrait of the dying days of the 'Merchant Navy' Pacifics on the Southern: No 35008 (formerly *Orient Line*) prepared to restart the 6.35pm Salisbury-Waterloo service out of Basingstoke on 5 July 1967. The first of the class of 30 air-smoothed Bulleid locomotives to be rebuilt was No 35018 in 1956, the entire class being so treated by 1959.

Right:
Destined to be one of the last examples of the dwindling band of Bulleid 'Austerities', Class Q1 0-6-0 No 33027 trundles into Basingstoke with an assorted freight for the Southampton line on 14 August 1965. The fitted vans at the head of the train are empty banana vehicles bound for the Docks. *G. D. King*

Centre right:
Heading west into the prevailing wind and rain, 'Battle of Britain' Pacific No 34064 *Fighter Command* was obliged to wait at Basingstoke for a clear road while working an afternoon train to Salisbury on 7 April 1966. This particular locomotive was selected as the guinea pig for tests with a Giesl oblong ejector type of chimney, but steam bowed out before the experiment could be properly evaluated. *R. E. B. Siviter*

Right:
With the deep, measured exhaust beat associated with the large two-cylinder 4-6-0s operated by the Southern, Class H15 No 30476 restarted its relief boat train for Southampton Docks from Worting Junction, west of Basingstoke, on 16 July 1960. Set No 440 comprised 10 corridor carriages of Maunsell origin, thus giving the entire train a period flavour of the 1930s. *Derek Cross*

Above left:
Leaning to the curve of the remodelled trackwork in readiness for electrification, 'Merchant Navy' No 35013 *Blue Funnel* thunders through Micheldever with the 1.30pm Waterloo-Weymouth service on 18 March 1967. The trackless Down platform and canopy have since been demolished, but the original Up station building has been retained as an example of London & Southampton Railway architecture; the station opened on 11 May 1840 as Andover Road. *John H. Bird*

Below left:
Until 1957 Alton-Winchester services were normally in the hands of push-pull trains powered by a Drummond 'M7' tank, after which two-car Hampshire DMUs became the norm until closure of the Mid-Hants route in 1973. However, the track was suitable for diversions when the main line via Basingstoke was closed — it was used by the heaviest trains on a number of occasions prior to the completion of main line electrification. On 1 May 1966 the 10.30am Waterloo-Weymouth service travelled that way with rebuilt 'Merchant Navy' No 35008 *Orient Line* in charge. The locomotive was hard at work on the ascent from Alton to Medstead & Four Marks when recorded from the lineside. *W. G. Sumner*

Above right:
In the summer of 1966 one or two visiting Stanier 'Black 5s' were pressed into service on the Southern. For example, on 15 May No 45493 (complete with SR headcode discs) was put in charge of the 8.55am Bournemouth Central-Waterloo train. This interesting combination ran via Ropley station on the Mid-Hants single line due to pre-electrification engineering work around Basingstoke; the scene makes a fascinating contrast with today's preservation activities at this location. *J. Scrace*

Right:
Just one of the 20 Class 3 2-6-0s constructed under the BR Standard steam programme reached the Southern. No 77014 powered the weed-killing train when it visited the Mid-Hants line on 28 July 1966, working hard on the adverse grade at the approach to Medstead & Four Marks station, through the deep cutting.
J. H. Bird

Above:
As a welcome change from Hampshire DEMUs on local services, diverted trains to Waterloo operated via the Mid-Hants line on 15 May 1966. The 9.54am from Weymouth featured Standard Class 4 No 80151 in tandem with air-smoothed 'West Country' Pacific No 34019 *Bideford*, seen passing Itchen Abbas station before attacking the steepest gradient beyond Alresford as far as Medstead & Four Marks. *J. Scrace*

Below:
Passing the site of the former goods yard at Itchen Abbas, the oldest 'West Country' Pacific in original condition (No 34002 *Salisbury*) drifts by some charming cottages with the 11.30am Waterloo-Weymouth train on 1 May 1966. The train was diverted 'over the Alps' because of engineering works at Micheldever on the main line. *J. H. Bird*

Above:
With Eastleigh Works just visible beyond the signals on the left, Class N 2-6-0 No 31825 steadily draws away from the South Junction box with freight for Fratton yard one January day in 1954. The Southern acquired no less than 80 of these rugged two-cylinder mixed-traffic engines for use all over the system; one has been saved from scrap, and may now be seen on the Mid-Hants line between Alresford and Alton.
L. Elsey

Below:
The gloomy, forbidding aspect of the old Down platform at Eastleigh contrasts with the sparkling condition of 'King Arthur' class 4-6-0 No 30783 *Sir Gillemere* as it draws into the Up platform with the Bournemouth-Bradford through service on 21 June 1952. The train consists of set 440, a mixture of LSWR 'Ironclad' coaches and Maunsell stock, one of which is painted in the shortlived 'Plum and spilt milk' colours inspired by the London & North Western Railway.
G. H. Robin

Left:
For several years after Nationalisation, elderly 'M7' 0-4-4Ts continued to appear on main line local trains. No 30378 had more than 200 tons behind the bunker one fine afternoon in September 1951 as it passed some wartime sidings between Eastleigh and Swaythling with a service for Southampton Terminus. Note the lack of emblem on the side tanks, a temporary expedient resorted to soon after a BR livery was first agreed upon. *P. Ransome-Wallis*

Centre left:
One of the lively little Class 2 2-6-2T locomotives allocated to the Southern, No 41305, bursts beneath Campbell Road bridge at Eastleigh with a rake of Maunsell carriages forming the 3pm to Fawley on 28 October 1960. Few passenger trains served Fawley; despite dieselisation using Hampshire DEMUs the facility was withdrawn in February 1966. *Bryan H. Kimber*

Below:
The changing face of Southampton can be discerned in this 1966 view at Swaythling. 'West Country' 4-6-2 No 34040 *Crewkerne* hustles northwards with an Up express for Waterloo past the redundant signal cabin and abandoned goods yard, while a typical 1960s monstrosity in the shape of a tower block of flats has been erected overlooking the main line. *A. D. McIntyre*

Right:
With smoke and steam erupting skywards in the crisp atmosphere, rebuilt 'Battle of Britain' Pacific No 34088 *213 Squadron* has some difficulty coming to grips with the combined Brighton and Portsmouth-Plymouth train when restarting from Fareham on 1 January 1962. Including a restaurant car, the gross load must, have been in excess of 350 tons — a formidable task for one of Bulleid's notoriously footloose creations at any time, let alone in conditions of frost and snow!

Below:
On summer Saturdays the 12.15pm from Portsmouth & Southsea ran as a separate train throughout (not combining with the Brighton-Plymouth service at Fareham) and was extended to Ilfracombe for the benefit of West Country holidaymakers. On 10 August 1957 Class U 2-6-0 No 31637 cautiously negotiated the bridge across the River Hamble at the approach to Bursledon when in charge of the Ilfracombe train, the nine-coach load being close to the limit for this type of engine over this difficult route. *E. Wilmshurst*

Left:
With a mixed bag of vans forming the 8.30am from Northam yard to Fareham, Standard '4MT' 2-6-0 No 76066 swept round the curve past Butlocks Heath between Netley and Hamble on 28 October 1966. While a branch from Portswood (now St Denys) was opened as far as Netley for the Royal Victoria Hospital in 1866, it took a further 23 years before a link was constructed eastward via Bursledon and Swanwick to Fareham, providing a direct connection between the two great towns of Southampton and Portsmouth. *J. H. Bird*

Below:
Not long before being withdrawn for preservation as part of the National Collection, air-smoothed Light Pacific No 34051 *Winston Churchill* was employed on a Bristol (Temple Meads)-Portsmouth train, passing through Netley station on 6 June 1965. The usual motive power on such services was a Standard '4MT' 2-6-0 or 4-6-0, or a Maunsell 'U' class 2-6-0. *Joma Enterprises*

Above:
The end of an era was reached on 3 February 1967, when the 8.30am parcels train from Northam yard to Fareham was operated for the last time, since it was one of the few remaining steam duties over the Netley line. Standard Class 4 2-6-4T No 80139 was the engine, entering Woolston with the cylinder cocks open — the River Itchen with its twin floating bridges still providing a link with the Southampton shore in the distance. *J. H. Bird*

Below:
Western Region 0-6-0 No 3211 plods along tender-first by the River Itchen between St Denys and Northam with a semi-fitted freight from Eastleigh in early November 1960. Passenger services over the DN&S line ceased in March of that year, but freight continued to use the route until August 1964; Bar End yard, near Winchester (Chesil), remained in operation for a further couple of years. *Bryan H. Kimber*

Left:
Regularly employed at Winchester City and in Southampton Docks until 1963, Class B4 0-4-0T No 30096 was then sold to Corralls for further service at Dibles Wharf, Southampton. One morning in March 1968 the 1893-built survivor was fussily shunting BR 16-ton steel wagons across Dock Road in Southampton between Northam yard and the coal wharf while traffic waited in both directions. The Dibles Wharf line was the last of three 'tramways' serving the Itchen wharves; the engine was bought for restoration in 1972 and is now preserved in working order on the Bluebell Railway.

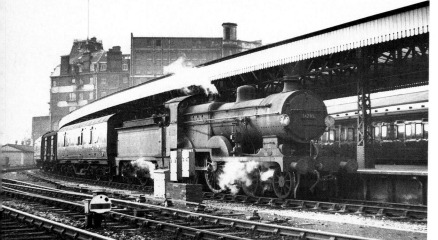

Left:
Banished from its native Kent and nearing the end of its days, Class D1 4-4-0 No 31735 occupied the outer bay platform at Southampton Terminus on 4 February 1961 with the 10.57am Salisbury-Portsmouth & Southsea vans. As the engine had arrived chimney first from Salisbury, it was necessary for it to be turned either on the small turntable adjacent to the Terminus station or on the Northam triangle before continuing its journey. *J. C. Haydon*

Left:
The Canute Road level crossing at Southampton, where trains entered or left the Old (Eastern) Docks, was a favourite location. On 29 September 1966 a Shaw Saville Line boat train for London (Waterloo) eased out of the Docks behind Standard Class 5 4-6-0 No 73022 while hand-signalmen straddled the road.

The Old Docks were a maze of sharply curved sidings serving quays and wharves dating back to Victorian times. Although Adams' 'B4' 0-4-0Ts were no strangers to Southampton Docks, since many had first seen service there in the 1890s, from 1946 they had been displaced by almost new 0-6-0Ts of American design, brought over for the war effort. By the 1950s and early 1960s the volume of traffic handled in both the Old and New Docks was such that some additional motive power was required; the spare engine retained for Winchester City shunting was often deployed in the Old Docks instead of remaining idle on shed at Eastleigh. On 9 June 1961 No 30096 trundled sedately through the area with an unfitted van kept for internal use.

With conductor rails already in position, 'West Country' Pacific No 34006 *Bude* dives beneath the girder road bridge at Northam on 16 September 1966 with a train from Waterloo. Note the four-wheeled van behind the tender. Both Northam and Southampton Terminus had closed a few days earlier, though the tracks to the Eastern Docks remain available for traffic. *D. A. Davies*

Above:
Emerging from the tunnel with a Portsmouth-Cardiff General service, Class U 2-6-0 No 31795 was approaching Southampton Central station on 23 June 1962. The tunnel itself was constructed in 1847 to link the Southampton & Dorchester Railway ('Castleman's Corkscrew') to the rest of the LSWR. *Michael J. Fox*

Below:
Southampton in transition: with the closure of the Terminus, major rebuilding was being undertaken at the Central station in preparation for electrification. On 25 October 1966 Class WC 4-6-2 No 34015 *Exmoor* passed through platform 3 with a fitted freight, while most of the former structure — including the clock tower — had been demolished on platform 1, beyond. *J. A. M. Vaughan*

Right:
From the public footbridge to the east, fine views could be obtained of much of the activity at Southampton Central station. On 3 August 1963 interest was centred upon the imminent departure of rebuilt 'Battle of Britain' 4-6-2 No 34090 *Sir Eustace Missenden, Southern Railway* **with the 11am Weymouth-Waterloo service from platform 2; the position of the headcode discs would appear to be suspect, however.** *R. A. Panting*

Right:
In the final summer before Nationalisation, Southern Railway 4-6-0 No 851 *Sir Francis Drake* **drew out of platform 4 at Southampton Central with the Saturday 2.13pm Waterloo-Bournemouth service on 5 July 1947. The engine was painted in Bulleid's Malachite green livery and still equipped with snifting valves at this stage.**
Pursey C. Short

Right:
This historic picture recalls both the final few months of steam on the Southern together with the impending departure of RMS *Queen Mary* **on her last voyage before preservation in America. Class 5MT 4-6-0 No 73043 was accelerating the 1.30pm Waterloo-Bournemouth service between Millbrook and Redbridge on 25 January 1967 while the famous Cunard liner was berthed in Southampton's Western Docks.**
D. Mackinnon

Above:
After the withdrawal of Drummond's doughty 'D15s', the mantle of summer boat trains to Lymington fell upon the 'Schools' 4-4-0s, since nothing bigger could be accommodated on the turntable at Brockenhurst. Class V No 30902 *Wellington* made a stirring departure from Southampton Central on Saturday, 28 July 1962 at the head of the 12 noon Waterloo-Lymington Pier boat train. 1962 was to prove the type's swansong year. *R. A. Panting*

Below:
Against the backdrop of Southampton's changing skyline Class 5MT 4-6-0 No 73083 (formerly *Pendragon*) lifted a Waterloo-Bournemouth relief out of Central station on 27 August 1966. An early Bulleid carriage from a three-coach 'shortie' set was coupled behind the tender, the Southern's tradition of established rakes of stock into particular sets having been discarded by this period.
J. A. M. Vaughan

Above:
A very clean rebuilt Pacific, No 34016 *Bodmin*, settles into its stride as it heads westward between Millbrook and Redbridge with a Waterloo-Bournemouth service in the early months of 1963. This locomotive was recovered from Barry scrapyard and restored to active use on the Mid-Hants Railway. *M. J. Esau*

Centre right:
Under storm clouds the 11.10am Bournemouth-Waterloo service sweeps round the curve at Redbridge behind Standard Class 5 4-6-0 No 73159 on 18 June 1966. Alongside, the sleeper depot's resident shunter, 'USA' class 0-6-0T No DS233, stands near its shed to await further activity. Formerly numbered 30061, this was the only example of the 14 working American-built tanks acquired by the Southern after the war to have been assembled by Porter rather than Vulcan. *J. H. Bird*

Below right:
Amid the industrial scene west of Southampton, Standard Class 4 2-6-4T No 80037 hustles six Maunsell corridor coaches forming the 12.50pm from Eastleigh to Wimborne (via Bournemouth Central) service towards Redbridge on 20 August 1960. The engine was an unusual visitor to the area, having a 74A (Ashford, Kent) shedplate. *J. C. Haydon*

Basingstoke to Andover along with the Test Valley Line

While still named the London & Southampton Railway, Basingstoke opened for business on 10 June 1839 as the temporary western terminal of the route from Nine Elms. Within a year trains were able to continue through the chalk downs to Winchester and Southampton, but already sights were set on further extensions westwards. By 1847 the junction at Bishopstoke (Eastleigh) had spawned a second branch — the first had opened to Gosport in 1841/42 — which meandered through Chandler's Ford to Romsey and thence via Dunbridge and Dean to Salisbury (Milford). A much more direct line to Salisbury via Andover came to fruition a decade later. But the London & South Western Railway, as the system had renamed itself, was being challenged by the Great Western, first at Basingstoke when a broad gauge branch from Reading was constructed in 1848, then at Salisbury (Fisherton). The LSWR began using the present Salisbury sta-tion, which straddles Fisherton Street along-side the former GWR terminus, in 1859; the Milford site became a goods depot, lasting as such until 1967.

Once plans to extend the Southampton & Dorchester Railway westward failed to find favour, the most natural course was to push on towards Exeter from Salisbury. But some infilling of the wide open spaces seemed prudent if the GWR was not to burst through with proposals of its own: from 6 March 1865 the Test Valley line linked Redbridge (on the Southampton & Dorchester route) with Romsey and Andover, utilising part of the former canal. Twenty years later a 'cut-off'

Below:
In the final days of steam on the Southern, rebuilt 'Battle of Britain' 4-6-2 No 34052 (formerly *Lord Dowding*) appears at the head of an assorted van train for Basingstoke from Salisbury beneath Battledown flyover. The gleaming paint-work indicates its use on a railtour recently, in contrast to the run-down condition so prevalent at the time. *J. L. McIvor*

route avoiding Andover was opened between Hurstbourne (on the West of England main line) and Fullerton, north of Romsey, but by then the heyday of railway construction was past and it was destined — like the Meon Valley line of 1903 — to remain forever a rural backwater. Nevertheless, at the time of its construction, prospects for the Test Valley route were sufficient to warrant realignment of the formation and provision of double track throughout between Redbridge and Andover Junction. No doubt some of the optimism was inspired by opportunities for through traffic via Cheltenham over the Midland & South West Junction Railway, encouraged by the entrepreneurial talents of one Sam Fay. This faith was not entirely misplaced, for there was some through passenger traffic from the Midlands and North to Southampton before World War 1, while in times of conflict (even as recent as World War 2) the route was extremely useful for the transportation of military equipment, troops and supplies. But, as with the parallel Didcot, Newbury & Southampton route, the line was allowed to stagnate postwar and Nationalisation handed most of the track north of Andover to the successors of the

GWR! The cross-country line between Cheltenham and Ludgershall was closed entirely in September 1961, while a similar fate befell the Kimbridge Junction-Andover Town section three years later; the branch from Fullerton had been severed north of Longparish many years before and was closed to the remaining freight traffic at the end of May 1956. There could scarcely be greater contrasts between the formidable quantities of traffic over the West of England line at Andover Junction and, say, the Test Valley route and former M&SWJR line at right angles to it: on summer Saturdays in the 1950s the former had its main train, the 'Atlantic Coast Express', running in several portions while the latter offered a haphazard service of local trains plus one through working between Southampton (Terminus) and Cheltenham. In the 1960s the Beeching axe

Below:
Leaning to the curve, the imposing bulk of 'H15' 4-6-0 No 30334 trundles a load of empty ballast hoppers towards the Battledown flyover west of Basingstoke on a fine September day in 1952. With their vast 'Watercart' tenders, the clutch of 'H15s' nominally rebuilt from Drummond 4-6-0s (Nos 30330-35) were all based at Salisbury (72B) for duties on the West of England route. *Brian Morrison*

Left:
On a crisp winter morning, Standard Class 4 2-6-0 No 76060 provided fine audio-visual effects as it attacked the 1 in 194 up from Hurstbourne at the approach to Whitchurch North station with an eastbound freight on 6 February 1960. The usual motive power for goods trains on the West of England main line was an 'S15' 4-6-0.

Below:
As the autumn evening was drawing in, 'Merchant Navy' 4-6-2 No 35023 (formerly *Holland Afrika Line*) set out for London from Andover Junction with an enthusiasts' special that had just visited the Ludgershall branch on 9 October 1966. At one time this had been a more important junction for cross-country routes, but closure of both the Midland & South Western Junction route beyond Ludgershall and the line from Romsey robbed it of much significance.

bit deep; while the West of England main line survived, the north/south route vanished from the map. The only section of it to survive is now under military control, from Andover Junction to Ludgershall. In the 1980s it enjoyed a few weekends of fame when public steam-hauled specials were operated, but these have yet to be repeated.

Hampshire's youngest railway is the branch from Totton to Fawley, but it has always been somewhat obscure due to the fact that there were few passenger services preceding their withdrawal in February 1966. The primary reason for the line since Nationalisation has been bulk oil traffic from the refinery at Fawley, though there may be periodic interchange at Marchwood of military freight to or from Cracknore Hard. In steam days it was the unique preserve of tank engines owing to the lack of turning facilities for tender engines and a host of ungated level crossings along the single-track route. A passing loop was added at Marchwood in 1960, but no extra platform was provided, so it could be used solely for freight trains.

The branch opened under the auspices of the Southern Railway on 20 July 1925, the mainstay of traffic being the 'M7' 0-4-4T. As oil trains became heavier, a trio of ex-LBSCR Class E6 0-6-2Ts was transferred to Eastleigh to handle them. In the early 1950s the trio was displaced by some new Ivatt Class 2 and Standard Class 3MT 2-6-2Ts, but double-heading had to be resorted to with fully-laden oil tankers from Fawley; engines were changed at Eastleigh or one of the Southampton area yards, a tender locomotive taking the train on to its destination. By 1960 the Southern Region was looking for something more powerful to tide matters over until diesel power could be made available — trials were held on 6 March (a Sunday) with one of the Urie 4-6-2Ts normally based at Feltham (70B). The 96-ton engine successfully handled a test train of coal wagons loaded up to 750 tons, with the result that a pair of the Class H16 tanks took up residence at Eastleigh specifically for the Fawley oil trains. By 1962 some of the three-cylinder Class W 2-6-4Ts had been displaced from the London area and lent a hand, although double-heading with one or other of the 2-6-2T classes remained commonplace until the diesels took over. Prior to the passenger services being worked by a spare DMU, it was not unknown for the Up morning train to be headed by an 'H16' — 'super-power' indeed for a three-coach local service.

Above:
Although some rationalisation of the M&SWJR route eliminated the Savernake (High Level) station in favour of the former GWR one at the Low Level, a Sunday service was retained between Swindon Junction and Andover Junction; this was especially popular with enthusiasts who wished to visit Swindon Works. One Sunday in July 1961, only a couple of months before withdrawal of passenger traffic, the first of the BR Standard Class 2 2-6-0 locomotives was rostered for the Sunday trains to and from Andover Junction. No 78000 was recorded coupled to a two-coach 'B' set in the loop platform 4, waiting to depart with the 12.40pm service to Swindon — a rare instance of one of these little mixed-traffic Moguls appearing at a Southern Region station.
G. Wheeler

Below:
During the course of a visit to the Bulford branch on 14 May 1955, this 1874-built 2-4-0WT, designed by Beattie but much rebuilt under successive CMEs at Eastleigh, reached Andover. Coupled to an appropriate ex-LSWR non-corridor set, No 30587 stood at the Junction station before shunting some other stock out of the loop platform. This elderly locomotive remained at work on the Wenfordbridge branch in North Cornwall until 1962, and is now preserved as part of the National Collection (outstationed at Buckfastleigh).
M. E. Ware

Left:
Although most passenger trains were covered by DMUs from November 1957, a handful of services were still the province of steam. Closure of the M&SWJR in September 1961 all but eliminated them, but the final steam working between Southampton, Romsey and Andover Junction occurred in 1962. Class N 2-6-0 No 31816 fulfilled the honours. It is seen on arrival at Andover Town.
R. I. D. Hoyle

Below:
Passenger services between Hurstbourne (on the main West of England line) and Fullerton Junction (on the Romsey-Andover line) were withdrawn in July 1931, though freight remained south of Longparish. The extremely rural nature of this truncated branch is evident in this study of Drummond 'Black Motor' 0-6-0 No 30306 drifting into the intermediate station of Wherwell with nothing but a brake van in tow on 17 August 1955.
J. H. Aston

Right:
One of the signal achievements of the M&SWJR was in linking Cheltenham and the Midlands with the burgeoning port of Southampton, to the chagrin of the rival GWR. After the Grouping the latter was empowered to operate the line. Something of this past connection was retained even in BR days, when Standard Class 4 2-6-0 No 76010 was entrusted with three ex-GWR corridor coaches forming the 10.10am from Southampton Terminus to Cheltenham Spa (St James), photographed beside the upper reaches of the River Test near Fullerton on 2 November 1957. *G. Daniels*

Right:
Typical of local passenger trains over the Test Valley route to Andover immediately prior to the introduction of DMUs is this combination of classic Drummond 'Greyhound' 4-4-0 and Bulleid corridor set. Class T9 No 30284 heads north between Horsebridge and Stockbridge with the 10.51am from Portsmouth & Southsea to Andover Junction on 2 November 1957. *G. Daniels*

Right:
Headed by one of the stalwarts of the cross-country route to Salisbury, Class 4 2-6-0 No 76005, the 4.45pm service from Portsmouth & Southsea arrives at Dunbridge on 7 September 1957. Nowadays this station is called Mottisfont Dunbridge, to reflect its proximity to the long-closed station of Mottisfont on the erstwhile Test Valley route between Romsey and Andover Junction.
J. Spencer Gilks

Above:
Striding along in classic style, 'H15' 4-6-0 No 30475 brings a Salisbury-Eastleigh goods towards Halterworth level crossing on the Romsey-Chandler's Ford section. Passenger trains were withdrawn from this line in 1969 and the route singled as an economy measure, although it is still open for freight traffic and diversions if required. *L. Elsey*

Below:
The 2.20pm local from Romsey to Eastleigh coasted into the intermediate station of Chandler's Ford on 7 September 1957 consisting of a set of three ex-LSWR non-corridor coaches and a contemporary 'M7' 0-4-4T No 30130. This useful little station was closed in 1969, since when there has been much development in the area; maybe the station will be reopened in the 1990s? *J. Spencer Gilks*

Above:
Numerically the last of the 'King Arthur' class of 4-6-0s, No 30806 *Sir Galleron* picks up speed with a load of hopper wagons passing Eastleigh East on 2 March 1960. This was one of the engines made redundant by the Kent Coast electrification of 1959, being transferred to the Western Section to eke out its final days on duties such as this. The six-wheel tender was also replaced by a secondhand bogie pattern, probably from another member of the class which had been already scrapped. *L. Elsey*

Below:
Freight traffic for the Eling tramway, Totton and the Fawley branch was handled by a succession of tank locomotives throughout the BR steam era. Three ex-LBSCR Class E6 0-6-2Ts were displaced by a handful of the new Standard Class 3 2-6-2Ts, and these were supplemented by Ivatt '2MTs' in due course. On a rarely photographed section of the branch, Standard Class 3 No 82012 coasts towards Hythe with an Eastleigh-Fawley freight, with not a tank wagon in sight, on 3 April 1953. *L. Elsey*

Passenger services to Fawley were few and far between. There was a Saturdays only train from Southampton Central at 4.14pm, which might be double-headed to avoid light engine movements on the single-track branch south of Totton, the spare engine then being employed for shunting or to help with freight traffic. On a September day in 1952 a brace of Drummond 'M7' 0-4-4Ts, Nos 30030 and 30029, appeared on this service. They were coupled chimney-to-chimney with a non-corridor set calling at all stations to Fawley. *N. Craig*

Two of the 'USA' 0-6-0Ts purchased for use in Southampton Docks were in double-harness for the LCGB tour of Hampshire branch lines on 9 April 1967. Coupled bunker-to-bunker to please photographers, No 30069 was leading No 30064 for the outward journey to Fawley when pictured south of Marchwood.

A somewhat humble task for such a fine locomotive, 'West Country' 4-6-2 No 34038 *Lynton* shuffles away from Redbridge station with a stopping train for Bournemouth on the morning of 23 December 1961. The shunting neck of the sleeper depot is on the right.

Above:
As part of the ongoing upgrading of the Waterloo-Bournemouth route prior to electrification, a new viaduct over the Test estuary was constructed during the winter of 1963/64. On 31 May 1964 rebuilt 'Merchant Navy' 4-6-2 No 35011 *General Steam Navigation* slowly headed eastward, wrong road, over the old viaduct on its last day; later, the new viaduct was commissioned for use by service trains. No 35011 was working the Sunday 10.26am train from Bournemouth West to Waterloo. *M. J. Fox*

Below:
Inter-Regional services sometimes brought visiting locomotives to the south coast. On 16 July 1964 it was the turn of 4-6-0 No 6978 *Haroldstone Hall* to bring the daily Newcastle-Bournemouth train over the new Redbridge viaduct. The train comprised Southern stock, including an augmented Bulleid set (No 836). Behind the semi-open brake at the front of the set can be seen the remains of the old viaduct with 'USA' 0-6-0T and bolster wagons recovering materials. *M. J. Fox*

Left:
An historic picture of the original Redbridge viaduct dating from the early postwar years; air-smoothed 'Merchant Navy' No 21C18 *British India Line* was recorded steaming westward with a 12-coach rake of Maunsell corridor coaches behind the tender bound for Bournemouth. This locomotive was the first to be rebuilt in 1956 — as No 35018 is today under restoration at Ropley on the Mid-Hants Railway. *Frank F. Moss*

Left:
On a still winter day an unrebuilt Bulleid Pacific leaves a trail of white smoke and steam after crossing the new Redbridge viaduct with the 11.30am Waterloo-Bournemouth service. No 34102 *Lapford* was the locomotive and the date was 30 December 1966. *J. H. Bird*

Left:
An evocative scene at Redbridge: Class U 2-6-0 No 31639 brings an engineers' train bound for Eastleigh from the Bournemouth line over the old viaduct across the mouth of the River Test during the evening of 21 May 1962. *M. J. Fox*

Brockenhurst to Lymington and a choice of routes to Bournemouth

The opening of the Southampton & Dorchester Railway in 1847, worked by the LSWR, was to lay the foundations for a major rail link between London and the new, fashionable resort amid the pine trees on the Hampshire/Dorset border. At first, the nearest station was at Hamworthy (but called Poole), the terminus of a short branch from the main line at what is now Hamworthy Junction, on the western shore of Poole Harbour. Fifteen years later another branch was opened from Ringwood via Hurn to Christchurch but, even then, it was not long before local enterprise was offering connections by horse-bus from Holmsley directly to Christchurch and Bournemouth that were quicker than by rail. The LSWR extended its branch to Bournemouth East in 1870, but a further opportunity arose to serve the Westbourne district with a new terminus in

concert with the Somerset & Dorset in 1874. This entailed descending steeply from Broadstone to present-day Poole before climbing equally steeply to Parkstone and Branksome on the way to Bournemouth West. Finally, realising that the 1847 route — nicknamed 'Castleman's Corkscrew' after the solicitor who promoted the line — was not as direct as the more discerning members of the travelling public would like, the LSWR bit the bullet and constructed a new railway

Below:
Class 'A' headlamps (WR-style) proclaim this to be an inter-Regional service. 'Hall' class 4-6-0 No 7905 *Fowey Hall* **justifies the super-elevation at Lyndhurst Road station as it storms through with the York-Bournemouth train on 2 May 1963. The sparkling condition of the locomotive, with its burnished Brunswick green paintwork and copper-capped chimney, reflects great credit to its home shed of Banbury (84C).** *M. J. Fox*

through Sway, New Milton and Hinton Admiral to Christchurch in 1888. Meanwhile an imposing through station had been opened on 20 July 1885 at Bournemouth Central to replace the short-lived terminus at Bournemouth East; this allowed lines to be laid to link up Central with Bournemouth West, so providing two alternative routes and plenty of flexibility in their operation.

After the huge expansion of lines worked by the LSWR in 1847, to Salisbury and Dorchester respectively, some thought was given to linking them by a chord that was, in effect, the third side of a rather unequal triangle. The first step was taken by an independent concern in December 1866 opening a single line from Alderbury Junction (between Salisbury and Dean) to West Moors, east of Wimborne on the 'Corkscrew' route; later it was absorbed into the parent system. Together with the easternmost section of the 'Corkscrew', from Lymington Junction as far as Broadstone, this line was closed from 4 May 1964.

The LSWR seemed to have a 'nose' for building or acquiring lines that connected with ferries, especially those to the Isle of Wight, so it was not surprising to find the company involved in the branch to Lymington — a ferry from there to Yarmouth on the Isle of Wight had begun in 1830. The impressive station at Lymington Town was brought into use in 1860, though services from Brockenhurst to a temporary terminal appear to have been inaugurated before then. While the Town station really was quite close to the main street, it was on the wrong side of the

river for the ferries. In due course the LSWR took over the steamer services to Yarmouth and, in 1884, extended the branch a further ½ mile to a new terminus at Lymington Pier, for the convenience of ferry passengers.

Bournemouth shed (71B) became responsible for most local workings in and out of Brockenhurst: in practice, this meant push-pull trains powered by the familiar 'M7' 0-4-4Ts operating both over the 'Old Road', as the 1847 'Corkscrew' route became known, and on the Lymington branch. Bournemouth-Salisbury local trains tended to be the preserve of older tender engines — four-coupled designs by Adams and Drummond were quite capable of keeping time with light loads well into their dotage on such a route. Matters became a little more complicated during the summer season, because the volume of extra traffic on Saturdays encouraged the timetable planners to look at under-used country lines as a means of absorbing some of the additional through trains. For example, the relative tranquillity of push-pull services over the 'Old Road' might be interrupted by a through express between London and Swanage, while the quiet by-way that ran beside the River Avon past Downton, Breamore and Fordingbridge could echo to the sound of a holiday train from Cardiff to Pokesdown. Lymington services could be disrupted by two or three Boat trains bound for London while, on the main line, upper-quadrant semaphores were forever being pulled off to signal yet another service between the capital and the coast. In steam days the variety of motive power was fascinating: in the early years of

Nationalisation a Marsh Atlantic of Class H2 could be anticipated on the through train from Brighton, and even until 1962 the four-coupled tradition might be maintained with a 'Schools' on this service. Their liveries, too, were a revelation, especially in the early years of British Railways, when Malachite green, Brunswick green and black vied for recognition beside the handful of blue 'Merchant Navy' Pacifics. A solitary 'Britannia' Class 7 4-6-2 (No 70009 *Alfred the Great*) worked the colourful 'Bournemouth Belle' Pullman for a time, then there was a brief season of strangers replacing the 'Merchant Navy' class, temporarily withdrawn for examination in 1953, that included ex-LNER 'V2s', 'B1s', ex-LMS 'Black Fives' and others. Then, as always throughout the year, the observer might be rewarded with something from the Swindon stable on an inter-Regional service, an object lesson in burnished copper and brass if one was fortunate. It should be remembered that the ex-GWR mixed-traffic 4-6-0s were painted in lined black livery until 1956/57, which tended to accentuate the polished metalwork when clean; the larger, purely passenger 4-6-0s which warranted Brunswick green paintwork were not supposed to work on to Southern tracks because of clearance problems with the outside cylinders. After 1956, of course, when Swindon relaxed the rules about application of green paint, practically anything might be adorned with it!

Below left:
One of the Bulleid Pacifics to remain in original air-smoothed state throughout its working life was No 34019 Bideford, recorded hustling a trainload of fitted cement wagons through the New Forest towards Brockenhurst on 7 August 1965. *K. R. Pirt*

Right:
Something of the enduring charm of the architecture of one of the original Southampton & Dorchester Railway stations may be discerned in this 1963 study of Beaulieu Road, doubtless enhanced by the sight and sound of rebuilt Bulleid Pacific No 34046 Braunton thundering through with a Waterloo-bound express one December afternoon.
Alastair D. McIntyre

Right:
As the sun was sinking in the western sky, rebuilt 'Battle of Britain' 4-6-2 No 34052 (formerly named Lord Dowding) raced across one of the clearings in the New Forest between Brockenhurst and Beaulieu Road with an Up express from Bournemouth on 21 January 1967. *Ian S. Krause*

Above:
The York-Bournemouth West through service drifted into Brockenhurst behind No 4979 *Wootton Hall* on Whit Monday 1959; at least one ER carriage was included in the stock, still painted in the early British Railways colours of crimson and cream. On the other face of the Down island platform stood some Maunsell carriages in Southern green. This scene was typical of the fascinating contrasts that could be found at this period. *Rimmer Industrial Photography*

Right:
One of the ex-LMR engines imported by the Southern to replace ageing Drummond 0-4-4Ts, Class 2 2-6-2T No 41224 replenishes its tanks before setting off from Brockenhurst with another branch train for Lymington Pier during August 1966. *J. M. French*

Above:
On summer Saturdays tender engines were to be seen handling long rakes of corridor carriages between Brockenhurst and Lymington in place of the usual push-pull set. On an overcast day, Class Q 0-6-0 No 30541 had run round at **Lymington Pier while passengers streamed on to the connecting ferry for Yarmouth (IOW). The locomotive then headed the 1.28pm Boat train for London (Waterloo), handing over to a 'Schools' class 4-4-0 at Brockenhurst for the sprint up the main line on 23 July 1960.**

Left:
Typical of the regime on the branch until 1964, when the elderly 'M7' tanks finally retired from their long-established push-pull duties, 0-4-4T No 30028 was propelling a pair of ex-LSWR 'Ironclad' brakes formed into a push-pull set in 1949 from Brockenhurst towards Lymington on 10 April 1960.
J. C. Haydon

Above:
Recalling visits by the class on summer Saturdays to deal with heavy holiday traffic, 'Q1' 0-6-0 No 33006 shuffles tender-first over the river bridge at Lymington between Pier and Town stations on 19 March 1966 with an enthusiasts' special. This was one of its final tasks before withdrawal, No 33006 being the last of these distinctive engines to remain in traffic. *W. G. Sumner*

Below:
On Saturday, 1 September 1962, Standard Class 4 2-6-0 No 76027 negotiated the viaduct over the Lymington river with the 1.28pm from the Pier terminus to Waterloo, hauling a Boat train of smart Bulleid corridor stock. The Mogul worked the service for the first five miles before handing over to another engine — most likely a 'Schools' 4-4-0 — for the remaining 92¾ miles to London. *M. J. Fox*

Providing its passengers with a leisurely ride through the New Forest, Class N 2-6-0 No 31408 restarts the 5.12pm from Southampton Terminus to Bournemouth at Sway station on 3 August 1965. The stock includes some ex-LMS corridors, perhaps pressed into service by the Southern pending a weekend holiday turn back to the Midlands.
A. D. McIntyre

Engineering works in the run-up to electrification of the Bournemouth main line created numerous problems for the traffic department.. With the original 'Castleman's Corkscrew' line through Ringwood and Wimborne closed in 1964, there was no alternative to the continued use of the 1888 route via Sway while the work was going on, so a single-line system was installed temporarily. On 25 March 1966 'West Country' 4-6-2 No 34024 was brought to a halt with the 3.35pm from Waterloo to allow Standard Class 4 No 80019 piloting a double-chimney 4-6-0 passage with the 5.40pm Bournemouth-Eastleigh through the bottleneck near Sway.
J. L. Murphy

Near Hinton Admiral one or two skew-arch bridges are a distinctive feature of the landscape. Class S15 4-6-0 No 30838 bustles along beneath one of them with the 5.5pm from Southampton Terminus-Bournemouth local service on 13 July 1964. The train comprises some maroon ex-LMS stock. *Carl Symes*

Above:
Always an awesome sight when at speed, the few remaining unrebuilt 'West Country' locomotives could be found on Waterloo-Weymouth services in the final months preceding electrification. No 34102 *Lapford* powered the 8.35am from London to Bournemouth through Hinton Admiral station on 1 September 1966 with appropriate carriages to match.
J. H. Bird

Below:
Effective panning produced this unusual picture of a dome-less Stanier Class 5MT 4-6-0 pressed into service with Southern stock on the long embankment between Hinton Admiral and Christchurch with a Down train for Bournemouth on 22 September 1966. The rather grimy No 45222 was coupled to a tender displaying the long-defunct initials of the London Midland & Scottish Railway for its brief visit to the south coast. *A. J. Dewis*

Above:
A charismatic 'Lord Nelson' 4-6-0 was in charge of the 1.22pm Waterloo-Bournemouth service on 18 July 1953. No 30861 *Lord Anson* drifted into Christchurch past the former junction for Hurn and Ringwood at the head of a selection of Maunsell stock. The signalbox and Up platform bracket signal provide period lineside detail at this historic location. *R. Goult*

Below:
The banked curve through Christchurch station provided the setting for this study of No 34106 *Lydford* when it passed through non-stop with a Waterloo-Bournemouth express on 8 April 1955. Built at Brighton Works in 1950, this particular 'West Country' was destined to have a working life of just 14 years and was scrapped in original air-smoothed condition. *D. M. C. Hepburne-Scott*

Above:
One of the early examples to be rebuilt from the original air-smoothed condition, 'Merchant Navy' 4-6-2 No 35014 *Nederland Line* recovers from a signal check at Christchurch as it crosses the River Stour with the Down 'Bournemouth Belle' on 13 April 1958. *C. P. Boocock*

Right:
When still quite new, Standard Class 4 2-6-0 No 76017 was recorded working a local passenger service between Bournemouth and Southampton on 21 May 1954. Running parallel with a gas-lit street, the mixed-traffic engine was accelerating away from Bournemouth Central with a four-coach train comprising a non-corridor ex-LSWR set and a Maunsell open third. After an eventful life, this locomotive is now restored to working order on the Mid-Hants Railway. *H. Gordon Tidey*

Left:
A fine summer morning found 'Lord Nelson' class 4-6-0 No 30864 *Sir Martin Frobisher* just getting into its stride with an Up London train leaving Bournemouth Central station. On 10 June 1953 No 30864 headed a mixed collection of carriages formed into set No 440, the brake behind the tender being of the LSWR 'Ironclad' style.
S. Rickard

Centre left:
A classic study of Bournemouth Central in prewar days, with one of the original Urie 'King Arthur' 4-6-0s about to leave for London one day in August 1936. Painted in Southern Railway olive green, the engine was No 753 *Melisande*.
Geoffrey J. Jefferson

Below left
On summer Saturdays some holiday trains for the south coast travelled by cross-country routes to avoid the congested main lines. On 3 September 1955 a through train from Cardiff General entered Bournemouth Central from the west, having travelled from Salisbury via Fordingbridge, West Moors and Poole behind Class Q 0-6-0 No 30543. This service terminated at New Milton station.
C. P. Boocock

Above right:
Standard Class 4 2-6-0 No 76006 had the task of disposing of the empty stock of the 10.30am from Waterloo on 16 August 1966. In the background was the locomotive depot at Bournemouth Central (71B), which survived until the very end of steam working on the Southern. *J. H. Bird*

Below right:
On 6 September 1966 an unpowered driving trailer in all-blue livery contrasted with the green engine and carriages forming the 11.25am Weymouth-Waterloo service at Bournemouth Central. With clear signals, rebuilt 'West Country' No 34013 *Okehampton* was about to creep forward with the Up express in the direction of Pokesdown. *J. Scrace*

Above left:
On the morning of 21 April 1954 the eastern end of Bournemouth Central station played host to a pair of Bulleid Light Pacifics. No 34105 *Swanage* had clear signals to depart with a school special from the main platform, while No 34064 *Fighter Command* waited in the bay to take over the 10.30am for London (Waterloo). *C. P. Boocock*

Below left:
In brilliant lighting conditions, the dramatic effect of steam could be seen at its best. 'Merchant Navy' 4-6-2 No 35018 *British India Line* has brought the Up 'Belle' in from

Bournemouth West and prepares to depart for London while 'King Arthur' class 4-6-0 No 30783 *Sir Gillemere* waits impatiently in the loop with a fitted freight on 17 August 1958. *C. P. Boocock*

Above:
As the day draws to a close, headlamps have been substituted for discs on Standard Class 5 4-6-0 No 73093, waiting at the Up platform of Bournemouth Central with a stopping service to Eastleigh on 4 March 1967. By this time the Up and Down loops had been removed, so that the trackwork resembles the layout in use today. *Verdun Wake*

Top:
In one of its last public appearances before withdrawal, Class M7 0-4-4T No 30480 was employed carriage shunting to the west of Bournemouth Central station on 25 April 1964. During much of the winter this veteran had plodded up and down the Lymington branch with a push-pull set or trundled round the 'Old Road' between Brockenhurst, Wimborne and Poole, but now the time had come for the last of Drummond's engines to bow out... *Ivo Peters*

Above:
Bournemouth West station was a major terminal for rail services from the Midlands and from London. A typical sight in the early 1960s was a Bulleid Pacific (in this case 'Battle of Britain' No 34053 *Sir Keith Park*) on a Waterloo-bound express and 'M7' 0-4-4T No 30127 carriage shunting. *Richardson Bros*

Right:
After closure of West station in September 1965, all trains used Bournemouth Central. Sole example of the Standard Class 3 2-6-0 to come south, No 77014, found employment with empty stock from Central on 8 July 1966 at Branksome; tracks from this station remained in place for the carriage sidings just to the north of the former Bournemouth West terminal. *Alastair McIntyre*

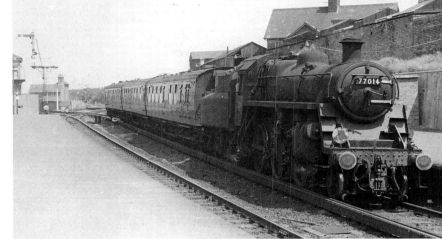

Right:
A striking portrait of a former star of the 'Pines' express, Standard Class 5 No 73051, battling with the ascent of Parkstone bank at the head of the 9.30am from Bristol (Temple Meads) to Bournemouth West on a December day in 1964.
Peter Walnes

Right:
An opportunity to see one of Drummond's classic 'Greyhound' 4-4-0s tackling Parkstone bank's notorious 1 in 60 gradient double-heading with 'West Country' 4-6-2 No 34106 *Lydford* occurred on 16 September 1956 when No 30727 was in pole position at the head of the 'Docks Express' excursion returning from Weymouth. *C. P. Boocock*

Above:
After the demise of the elderly LSWR 4-4-0s, most traffic between Bournemouth West and Salisbury was in the hands of 2-6-0s. On 31 March 1962 the 1.3pm service drifted downhill from Parkstone station with 'N' class No 31841 trailing a mere 100 tons behind the tender. The goods yard and headshunt are to the right of this picture. *M. J. Fox*

Left:
One of the push-pull sets (No 603), created by modifying Maunsell corridor coaches, arrives at Parkstone station on the August Bank Holiday Monday in 1962. With Class M7 0-4-4T No 30105 propelling at the rear, this is the 2.3pm service from Brockenhurst to Bournemouth via Ringwood and Wimborne. *M. Mensing*

Below left:
At Parkstone, goods traffic was exchanged between the private Potteries line and BR. In this picture, which dates from 26 April 1959, the delightful Peckett 0-4-0ST *George Jennings* was shunting in the station yard before returning to the Potteries through the woodland. With its dome gleaming in the sunshine, the locomotive was coupled to a former private owner wagon (the name 'Denby' was still visible on the wooden body) and a modern 16-ton steel-sided truck.
D. S. Millett

Above:
Quite regularly employed on S&D local trains between Templecombe and Bournemouth since the early 1950s, a 'Mickey Mouse' 2-6-2T brings six coaches into Parkstone station, midway up the bank from Poole. This particular engine, No 41223, was not a native of the line but had been transferred to the Southern when made redundant on the LMR.
Derek Cross

Right:
Generally local trains between Brockenhurst and Bournemouth via the 'Old Road' were push-pull operations. On this particular occasion, probably in the early 1960s, push-pull 'M7' 0-4-4T No 30104 was attached to a Maunsell three-coach corridor set (No 202) when it was recorded tackling the stiff ascent of Parkstone bank with a service for Bournemouth Central. *Ivo Peters*

Above:
Today there is an overbridge for road traffic, but in steam days Poole was bedevilled by two level crossings on the Parkstone side of the station that severely disrupted traffic — especially on summer Saturdays. Both level crossings are visible in this study of rebuilt Bulleid Pacific No 35014 *Nederland Line* as it gets to grips with the weight of an Up express for London on Whit Monday 1964. *E. Thomas*

Below:
The LSWR 0-4-4Ts of both Adams and Drummond design were primarily passenger engines, but light freight and shunting duties were sometimes allocated to them. In Poole yard, one of the non auto-fitted 'M7s', No 30112, was performing some shunting with gusto during the late afternoon of 28 April 1962, marshalling a train of cement wagons.

Above:
A less common location for photographs around Poole Harbour shows rebuilt 'West Country' No 34045 *Ottery St Mary* powering the 12.26pm local service from Bournemouth West to Brockenhurst near Creekmore Halt. The two carriages would normally form a push-pull set with a Drummond 'M7' 0-4-4T, but by this date (19 April 1964) scarcely any of the old Drummond tanks remained fit for traffic; in any event, this service was to be withdrawn the following month. *R. A. Panting*

Centre left:
Typical of the local service between Bournemouth, Poole, Wimborne and Ringwood for many years, both before and after Nationalisation, is this combination of push-pull set No 662 and 'M7' 0-4-4T No 30058. Having just left Creekmore Halt, the engine is propelling its train up the 1 in 75 of Broadstone bank with an afternoon service for Brockenhurst on 4 June 1960.

Below left:
While ascending Broadstone bank with the Bournemouth West-Brockenhurst push-pull service on 26 July 1961 it was possible to observe closely Maunsell 'Q' 0-6-0 No 30543 tackling the 10.10am freight from Dorchester South to Millbrook on a parallel track as far as Broadstone Junction. The freight was routed via the original 'Castleman's Corkscrew' across Upton Heath from Hamworthy Junction, a section of line bereft of regular passenger trains, but retained for summer traffic to Swanage.

Above:

A lengthy freight forming the 10.10am from Dorchester South to Millbrook creeps forward into platform 4 at Broadstone Junction behind Class Q 0-6-0 No 30543 to await a clear road on 26 July 1961. Beyond the distant road bridge the track to Hamworthy Junction had been singled, but part of the original Up line was retained as a siding for empty coaching stock in the summer.

Right:

After calling at Broadstone Junction with a local service from Brockenhurst, Class M7 0-4-4T No 30031 accelerated its push-pull set and extra luggage van away from platform 1 bound for Poole and Bournemouth on 26 July 1961. The covered footbridge spanning all four platforms was a feature of this station.

Above:
Less than a month before closure of the 'Old Road' between Broadstone Junction and Brockenhurst, Standard Class 4 2-6-0 No 76019 waits in the extensive yard at Wimborne with stock to form the 11.12am service to Bournemouth West.
W. G. Sumner

Below:
Recalling something of the line's former eminence, rebuilt 'West Country' 4-6-2 No 34031 *Torrington* hustles the 10.36am from Bournemouth Central to Waterloo through Wimborne on Sunday, 3 April 1960. Until 1888, when the more direct route through Sway was built, the so-called 'Castleman's Corkscrew' via Ringwood, Wimborne and Poole provided the only rail link from London to the new and fashionable resort amid the pine trees. *C. P. Boocock*

Above:
After closure of stations between Broadstone Junction and Brockenhurst (exclusive) in 1964, the 'Old Road' was abandoned as a through route. Freight traffic from the west as far as Ringwood remained for a while, but this petered out in the autumn of 1966. A final enthusiasts' special was run from London via Bournemouth Central on 16 October that year: the double-headed train was recorded as it passed slowly through Ashley Heath Halt, between West Moors and Ringwood, with Class 3 2-6-0 No 77014 leading tender-first and '4MT' 2-6-0 No 76026 coupled to the train.

Centre right:
With its double track and regular service of local trains, it was unthinkable that the 'Old Road' between Poole and Brockenhurst should close — but that was before Beeching... On a fine summer Saturday (4 June 1960) a typical push-pull entourage comprising set No 31 and 'M7' 0-4-4T No 30060 was saddled with towing a four-wheeled van to cope with the extra luggage encountered at such times. This morning service from Bournemouth to Brockenhurst was pictured leaving Wimborne.

Below right:
Even after closure of the line to all traffic, steam visited Ringwood again on 11 February 1967 for the purpose of recovering materials. The run-down condition of double-chimney Class 4 4-6-0 No 75077 was a sad sight as it stood in the platform of the station that had once been the junction for Christchurch and Bournemouth (East) via Hurn. *J. H. Bird*

91

Above:
The 5.20pm Salisbury-Bournemouth West service hurries south towards Verwood, with Standard Class 4 2-6-0 No 76011 trailing Bulleid corridor set No 860 as the shadows lengthen on 1 May 1960. In the course of its 38-mile journey, the train manages to travel through three different counties (one of them twice).

Left:
One of the last Drummond 'Greyhound' 4-4-0s to receive a general overhaul at Eastleigh Works, 'T9' No 30707 drifts into Verwood with steam to spare at the head of the 12.16pm service from Templecombe to Bournemouth via Salisbury on 25 July 1959. Services into Bournemouth from both Salisbury and Brockenhurst via Broadstone Junction were withdrawn from 4 May 1964.

Right:
Eager to be off, Class T9 4-4-0 No 30707 waits at Verwood station for the arrival of the 1.20pm Bournemouth-Salisbury local service with '4MT' 2-6-0 No 76026 in charge on 25 July 1959. Both platform starting signals were still lower quadrant, which gave added charm to this rural line.

Right:
On summer Saturdays the familiar pattern of local trains was supplemented by one or two through services from far afield. On 13 July 1963 Standard Class 4 2-6-0 No 76056 headed a train of maroon stock from Nottingham (Midland) to Bournemouth through Fordingbridge station without stopping. This was the last season when such services could use this route as it closed in May 1964.
M. J. Fox

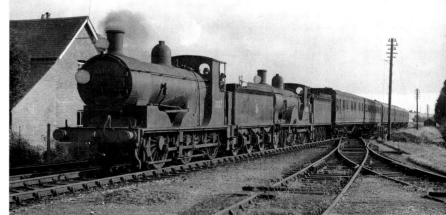

Right:
It was not uncommon for the late-afternoon service from Bournemouth to Salisbury to be double-headed. While in later years it might be a brace of Standard Class 4s, in the early years after Nationalisation it could produce a pair of Drummond veterans such as this: Class 700 0-6-0 No 30317 was piloting 'Greyhound' 4-4-0 No 30721 with the 4.47pm from Bournemouth West as it approached Downton station. The date was 18 July 1953. *S. C. Nash*

South and West from Templecombe and the Lyme Regis Branch

The West of England main line, west of Salisbury, dates from 1860. The same year saw the opening of the first stage of a famous cross-country route that was to link Bath with Bournemouth across the formidable Mendip Hills; the Dorset Central Railway, between Wimborne (on the 'Castleman's Corkscrew' route) and Blandford was operated by the LSWR from the beginning. When the Somerset Central, a broad gauge pawn of the Bristol & Exeter, amalgamated with the Dorset Central system in 1862, the idea was to link Burnham-on-Sea with Poole, but while this goal was achieved on the ground within a year of the establishment of the Somerset & Dorset Railway, it was soon overtaken in practice by the much more important connection via Bath and Evercreech Junction in 1874. The very real possibility of the Bristol

& Exeter — and thus the Great Western — taking over the complete system and so gaining a foothold on the South Coast at Poole and Bournemouth concentrated minds wonderfully, with the result that the entire S&D was leased by a consortium of the influential Midland Railway and LSWR combined, to be renamed the Somerset & Dorset Joint Railway to reflect the nature of its new ownership. Templecombe was to prove a pivotal point on the map, for it was there that the Salisbury and Yeovil route crossed the S&D at right angles; the opportunities for transfer of

Below:
Representative of S&D motive power in the last few years as a through route, Standard Class 9F 2-10-0 No 92006 raises the echoes when lifting the 3.40pm 'Postal' out of Bournemouth West on its way to Bath and Bristol during the summer of 1961. *R. Puntis*

Right:
The Up 'Pines Express' awaiting departure from Bournemouth West in August 1936; this famous train, which brought so many holidaymakers to the south coast resort and took them home again to the Midlands was headed on this occasion by a pair of Derby-built LMS Class 2P 4-4-0s (Nos 600 and 601). The Whitaker tablet exchange apparatus can be seen attached to the tender of each locomotive to assist with rapid negotiation of single-line sections experienced during the 71⅛ miles between Bournemouth and Bath. *G. J. Jefferson*

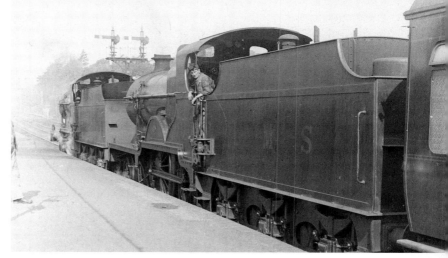

Right:
In the final season of through services over the S&D line there were regular appearances by the big '9F' 2-10-0s at weekends. No 92233 made a midweek visit and returned north with the 3.40pm 'Postal' on 11 July 1962, curving over one of Poole's notorious level crossings with Bulleid carriages behind the tender.
B. H. Jackson

Below:
Almost the end at Bournemouth West: a very scruffy Standard Class 5 4-6-0 (No 73001) pulls out with the 3.40pm to Bath (Green Park) on 12 June 1965. Within three months trains ceased to use the terminal station, being temporarily replaced by buses, before total closure in October 1965.
E. Tuddenham

passengers from one line to the other were too strong to be ignored. Apart from the natural cross-platform interchange, the facilities existed for actual operation of through carriages — a good example of this being between Cleethorpes, Sidmouth and Exmouth, a train that ran on Saturdays only during the summer of 1962, the final season in which through services were permitted to use the S&D line.

To return briefly to the establishment of the railway in the north and west of Dorset in its historical context, 1863 saw not just the inauguration of the S&D but also the opening of a branch from Chard Road (later Chard Junction) to Chard. This, and the associated GWR branch to Taunton, closed in September 1962, although Chard Junction station remained open for a further four years. Right on the Devonshire border, a branch was built in 1903 from Axminster to Lyme Regis under the auspices of the Light Railway Act, to be operated by the LSWR until it was fully absorbed in 1907. Initially, services were run with a pair of ex-LBSCR 'Terrier' 0-6-0Ts acquired specifically in view of the lightweight construction of the line, but once the LSWR took over fully more powerful locomotives were sought. The story of the Lyme Regis branch is, in reality, the remarkable tale of survival of two (finally three) of the 4-4-2T engines designed in the 1880s by William Adams, which lasted in traffic until 1961. The branch was closed, following a brief period with other types of steam locomotives and diesel railcar operation, at the end of November 1965.

The main line traversed no less than four counties on its way from Salisbury to Exeter: Wiltshire, Dorset, Somerset and Devon. It was engineered for speed, being famous for some remarkable exploits by steam engines over the years, from the prestigious Plymouth Boat trains of the Edwardian period to the 'Devon Belle' Pullman of the immediate post-war years. Drummond's 4-4-0 classes, despite their modest dimensions, gained respect for their ability to 'rush the banks' and maintain a good average speed over a switchback road; the rugged Eastleigh 'Arthurs' (BR Nos 30448-57) intensified the tradition until eclipsed by the unconventional Bulleid Pacifics. In the 1960s control west of Salisbury passed from the Southern to the Western Region, resulting in the partial singling of the line and its operation by 'Warship' diesel-hydraulic locomotives between Waterloo and Exeter St David's.

Yeovil was to prove the main focus for both GWR and LSWR activity along the county border. The broad gauge track of the former Bristol & Exeter Railway arrived on the outskirts of the town (at Hendford) in 1853, while another constituent of the Great Western reached Pen Mill station in 1856, being extended to Weymouth the following year; the link between Hendford and Pen Mill was opened shortly afterwards, although it was to be 1860 before the jointly-owned station at Yeovil Town was built midway between them, to mark the appearance of the LSWR on the scene. In the meantime, the LSWR opened throughout between Salisbury and Exeter via Yeovil Junction and tracks were laid around a great curve to connect Town and Junction stations. In due course the original spur from the LSWR main line to Yeovil Town was taken out of use, passengers changing at Yeovil Junction. The GWR made a foray from Pen Mill to a goods station alongside Yeovil Junction, known as Clifton Maybank, but it ceased to be used after 1937.

By Nationalisation the pattern of train services in the area had been established for many years: the Southern ran a push-pull 'shuttle' from Yeovil Junction to the Town station, providing connections with main line services to or from Salisbury (for London) and Exeter. A similar connection (but not always with an auto-train) linked the Town with Pen Mill for Western services to or from Weymouth, Castle Cary (for London Paddington) and Bristol (Temple Meads). Local trains from Pen Mill ran via the Town station northwestward to Taunton. Ex-GWR motive power for these consisted of 0-6-0PTs and various 2-6-2Ts (both large and small Prairies); in the 1960s these also included examples of the Standard Class 3 tank (in the 82xxx series). The Southern's contribution comprised a brace of 'M7' 0-4-4Ts, which took it in turns to operate the push-pull train; previously that had been the preserve of a motor-train 'O2' 0-4-4T. Some main line engines — 'S15' 4-6-0s, Class U or N 2-6-0s and the occasional Bulleid Pacific — might make transitory visits to the main shed (72C) which was located alongside Yeovil Town station. There was also a tiny WR sub-shed for one or two tanks near Pen Mill, in the 'V' between the single-track branch to the Town and the line to Weymouth, but it was later closed and the engines serviced at the main Southern shed.

Once the Beeching cuts started, Yeovil's local services fell like ninepins. First came closure of the branch to Taunton, withdrawn from June 1964 between Yeovil Town and Durston; then followed the connections between Town and Pen Mill in November 1965 and finally the end for the 'shuttle' from October 1966, with the Town station ceasing to have a railway function from 1 March 1967. For a time it continued to be used by Royal Blue coaches on express services to the West Country before even that came to an end.

Further east, the writing was on the wall for the Somerset & Dorset line once through passenger services were withdrawn at the end of the 1962 summer season. Purely local trains ran thereafter, until closure was scheduled for the beginning of January 1966. Even then it was reprieved for another couple of months, as replacement bus services had not been finalised! In retrospect, away from the understandable ill-feeling that closure — and its manner of attainment — brought about, BR did itself no favours by withdrawing the through services to Bournemouth via the S&D line without at least trying out more modern forms of motive power first; the experiments with the '9F' 2-10-0s were entirely successful, but any economies were allowed to 'wither on the vine'. Imagine how the S&D could have become a sort of southern Settle & Carlisle if its future had been safeguarded in the 1960s...

Right:
A dramatic view of Stanier Class 5MT 4-6-0 No 45440 rounding the sharp curve into Poole station with the 9.45am 'Pines Express' from Bournemouth West to Manchester in the early 1950s. The variety of motive power experienced in the Bournemouth area at this period, particularly in the summer, was quite remarkable.
O. J. Morris

Right:
Generally the preserve of a '4F' 0-6-0, on 11 June 1960 the 3.3pm freight for Templecombe was catered for by an S&D 2-8-0. Class 7F No 53807 had a particularly lightweight train as it got under way from Poole yard in bright sunshine. *J. C. Haydon*

Above:
With traditional S&D motive power, such as the 'Armstrong' Class 4Fs and the '7F' 2-8-0s, withdrawn, one of the last remaining freight services from Poole to Templecombe brought a BR-built example of a Swindon 0-6-0 to the line. On 8 June 1965 Class 2251 No 3218 swung across the points from Poole yard as it set out on its journey in dismal weather.
R. A. Panting

Left:
On Bank Holidays it was not uncommon for an excursion to run from Weston-super-Mare to Bournemouth via the S&D route. On 18 April 1960 the return excursion passed through Broadstone Junction behind one of the line's 'Armstrong' Class 4F 0-6-0s, No 44557, seen picking up the single-line tablet with its Whitaker patent apparatus on Easter Monday.

Above:

Exhibiting a non-authentic head-code, Class 9F 2-10-0 No 92209 brought an enthusiasts' special (the 'South Western Rambler') off the S&D line at Broadstone Junction into the Down Hamworthy platform on 8 March 1964. One of the station's two lower quadrant 'gallows' junction signals can be seen on the left; the train continued to Hamworthy Junction over the single line via Upton level crossing.

Right:

With steam to spare, Class 4F 0-6-0 No 44560 enters the final stretch of single line at Corfe Mullen signalbox when working the 12.23pm from Templecombe to Bournemouth West on 8 September 1962. This was the last day that through trains operated over the S&D from the Midlands and the North. The siding on the right was once the route to Wimborne (closed to passenger traffic in 1920 and freight in 1933).

Between Corfe Mullen signalbox and Blandford, the S&D was double-track. Though regularly employed on weekend passenger traffic involving through summer services from the Midlands and the North, Class 7F 2-8-0 No 53807 found itself working a Bournemouth-Bristol train (probably the 3.40pm 'Postal') on 3 July 1954. The location was north of Bailey Gate, near Spetisbury Halt. *R. E. Toop*

Charlton Marshall Halt was constructed in 1928 between Spetisbury and Blandford, but closed in September 1956. On 8 August 1959 an express bound for Bournemouth West hurried through, with 'West Country' 4-6-2 No 34105 *Swanage* coupled to a rake of ex-LMS coaches forming duty 'M223'. The engine may be seen today preserved in working order on the Mid-Hants Railway.

Above:
One hundred and two years after it opened for business as the northern terminus of the Dorset Central Railway, Blandford witnessed the last Down 'Pines Express' with *Evening Star* in charge on 8 September 1962. Class 9F 2-10-0 No 92220 had the distinction of being the final steam locomotive built for British Railways (at Swindon in 1960); it is now preserved as part of the National Collection, based at York.

Below:
At the north end of Blandford, the S&D line became single (with passing loops at certain stations) as far as Templecombe. On 23 September 1964 Class 4F 0-6-0 No 44422 was using the single track as a shunting neck, whilst rearranging wagons as part of the 3.3pm goods service from Poole. By late afternoon the deep cutting was always in shadow. *Peter Walnes*

Above:
By this late stage the goods yard was becoming overgrown and neglected, but 'Mickey Mouse' Class 2 2-6-2T No 41283 seemed in good form as it set off from Shillingstone with the 5.30pm Bournemouth-Templecombe local service on 16 July 1965. *Michael J. Fox*

Below:
As the shadows begin to lengthen, Ivatt Class 2 2-6-2T No 41243 busies itself with the 5.30pm from Bournemouth West to Templecombe on 17 August 1962. With a Bulleid short set (No 970) and van in tow, this typical local train over the southern half of the S&D is pictured in rural terrain between Shillingstone and Sturminster Newton. *G. A. Richardson*

Right:
In robust style, Standard Class 4 4-6-0 No 75072 storms past a PW hut at the lineside between Shillingstone and Sturminster Newton with the Up mail train (the 3.40pm from Bournemouth West) on 5 August 1960. *Richardson Bros*

Below:
One of the original S&D 0-6-0s, latterly numbered 44561, restarts the 4.16pm Evercreech Junction-Bournemouth West local service out of Stalbridge station, having waited there for the Up mail train for Bristol to pass on 28 March 1959. Whitaker patent tablet exchangers stand like sentinels on either side of the tracks to the south of the level crossing gates, while a fine old LSWR pattern bracket signal gives the authority to proceed.

Above:
Against the backcloth of the Southern's West of England main line, the first of the Derby-built Class 2Ps turned out under Fowler's direction in 1928 brings the 12.23pm local train from Templecombe southbound towards Henstridge on 20 March 1962. No 40563 must have been the last such 4-4-0 to be active on the S&D, for all the survivors were withdrawn during 1962.
Rev R. T. Hughes

Left:
Bursting from beneath the road bridge, 'Mickey Mouse' 2-6-2T No 41248 hustled through Templecombe (Lower) without stopping on 28 March 1959, with the 3.35pm service to Bailey Gate. Mainly intended for the milk traffic, the non-corridor train arrived at its country destination at 4.19pm. The only service regularly to use Templecombe's Lower platform was the 10pm from Bournemouth West, which ran on Saturdays only and terminated there to save shunting back into the Upper station.

Right:

In late afternoon sunlight, an assortment of S&D motive power was on display at Templecombe (71H) on 1 May 1958. While a local passenger train headed by a '2MT' 2-6-2T waited for admission to the Upper station on the embankment, one example of each of the tender locomotives could be seen around the shed building — '2P' 4-4-0 No 40563, '3F' 0-6-0 No 43216, a '7F' 2-8-0 and a '4F' 0-6-0. The S&D main line ran parallel to the shed below the embankment.
P. H. Wells

Right:

Accelerating rapidly past the shed yard at Templecombe, Standard Class 5 4-6-0 No 73050 heads south on 22 July 1961 with one of the many Saturday through trains for Bournemouth. Of the handful of the type sent to the S&D when new (to replace Stanier '5MTs') in the mid-1950s, No 73050 has been preserved and is now based on the Nene Valley Railway at Peterborough.

Right:

Passing Templecombe No 2 signalbox, '2P' 4-4-0 No 568 has the road to enter the Upper station with a local train from Bath (Green Park) on 30 June 1950. This period picture shows the engine — still exhibiting 22C shedplate — before BR renumbering, heading a set of ex-LSWR panelled corridor coaches past lower quadrant semaphore signals. *Ian Allan Library*

Top:
After the effort of pounding up the 1 in 100 gradient to Buckhorn Weston tunnel there is the relief of a similar gradient downhill towards Gillingham in prospect for the crew of 'S15' 4-6-0 No 30841 as it makes for Salisbury with a heavy goods on 2 June 1962. *G. A. Richardson*

Above:
The 11.30am Brighton-Plymouth through train has a temporary excess of steam as 'West Country' Pacific No 34096 *Trevone* makes a restrained departure from Templecombe on 26 July 1961. There has been an engine change at Salisbury (where the locomotive from Brighton is turned and serviced before returning east) and *Trevone* will take the train on to Exeter with only three intermediate stops.

Right:
An Up stopping service from Exeter Central keeps the power on up the 1 in 448 gradient towards Sherborne in the capable hands of Standard Class 5 4-6-0 No 73114 on 8 November 1958. A number of these Standard locomotives allocated to the Southern Region gained the names formerly carried by 'King Arthur' 4-6-0s; this one became *Etarre*. *B. A. Poley*

Right:
Yeovil was blessed with three stations: Town, Pen Mill and Junction. A regular shuttle was provided by the Southern between Town and Junction (where connections were made with the West of England main line services to Exeter or Salisbury/London), whereas a more sporadic timetable linked Town with Pen Mill (for connections to Weymouth or Bristol/Paddington via the Western Region). Typical of the Southern's contribution to these local services was Class M7 0-4-4T No 30131 and push-pull set No 373, last survivor of the LSWR 'gate' sets based on erstwhile steam railmotors from Drummond's day; this entourage was recorded setting out on another foray from Yeovil Town to Yeovil Junction on 3 August 1959, the elderly locomotive propelling in this direction.

Right:
On a bright December day in 1963 'Small Prairie' 2-6-2T No 5547 was engaged in some vigorous shunting at Yeovil Town, past the characteristic ring-arm lower quadrant signal and GWR notice beside the shunting neck. By this date the engine was in a shabby condition and had no front numberplate.

Above:
Full house at Yeovil Town: with frost clearing slowly in the shadows, WR 0-4-2T No 1451 and two auto-coaches wait to depart for Yeovil Junction as a Southern Mogul runs in alongside to go on shed. In the remaining platform a Standard Class 3 2-6-2T has the branch train for Taunton. Within three years this busy scene was no more, and it was not much longer before the fine old station — perhaps the most central site for passengers — was demolished to remain a wasteland in the heart of the town.

Below:
With the peace of Summer House Hill unruffled by an excess of steam from Bulleid Light Pacific No 34033 *Chard* as it prepared to go off shed at Yeovil Town, WR 0-6-0PT No 8745 waited for its next spell of duty at the end of a platform on 21 April 1962. These contrasting forms of motive power typified the joint nature of the Town station.

Above:

In headlong flight down the 1 in 80 (eased briefly to 1 in 250 through the station), *Brocklebank Line* **screamed a warning as it roared past Crewkerne box with the 7.30am Exeter-Waterloo express on 30 July 1960. It was here that another 'Merchant Navy' (No 35020** *Bibby Line***) had come to grief some years earlier, the incident leading to the rebuilding of the entire class plus half of the 110 Light Pacifics. No 35025 had a working life of just 16 years, being rebuilt in 1956 and withdrawn in 1964.**

Right:

On 3 August 1959 0-6-0PT No 7436 accelerated briskly away from Chard Central station with a Bank Holiday excursion from Ilminster to the coast. As interchange facilities at Chard Junction were primitive, involving shunting the train through the goods yard, it is probable that a Southern engine replaced the WR pannier tank there.

Above:
Burrowing beneath the main road through Chard, 0-6-0PT No 4663 and its obligatory 'B' set of non-corridor coaches forming the 4.7pm branch train to Chard Junction epitomise the charm of rural railways in the steam age. The date was 7 May 1960 — today no train serves the town and the cutting at this point has been filled in.

Below:
After turning away southwards, the Lyme Regis branch train was soon hard at work. Looking very smart in its lined-black livery, Class 0415 4-4-2T No 30582 swung elegantly round the many curves as it chugged steadily up the ruling 1 in 40 towards Combpyne with the 1.38pm from Axminster to Lyme Regis on 7 May 1960.

Above:
One-coach trains were not uncommon in certain parts of the southwest. Out of season, a single Maunsell brake composite was adequate to cater for passengers to Lyme Regis, as shown in this cameo portrait of ancient Adams' 'Radial'

No 30584 at Axminster in 1960. The branch had its own bay platform and trains climbed steeply to cross over the West of England main line, thereby avoiding conflicting movements that could delay passing traffic.

Above:
By 1961 the long reign of the Adams' 'Radial' tanks had come to an end; some realignment of the track at the most severe curves made it possible to use modern Class 2 2-6-2T locomotives instead. On 29 July No 41307 tackled the ruling 1 in 40 gradient unaided with a five-coach train conveying through carriages off the 10.45am London (Waterloo) service, bound for Lyme Regis.

Above:
The one intermediate station of Combpyne was effectively the summit of the branch. After pounding up 1 in 40 gradients in reverse gear, 'Radial' No 30582 paused for a few moments at the windswept platform with the 2.6pm Lyme Regis-Axminster train before descending to the junction with the West of England main line on 7 May 1960. In the siding stood an old LSWR panelled carriage used as a camping coach.

Below:
Alongside the attractive timbered terminal building at Lyme Regis, Class 0415 4-4-2T No 30583 paused for a moment before uncoupling and running-round its train on 3 August 1959. Part of this structure lives on, long after the branch closed, by being incorporated into an extension of the station at Alresford on the Mid-Hants Railway; the locomotive, also, survives in working order on the Bluebell Railway.

Poole to Purbeck and Portland

The modern Poole station lies on a great curve and, in steam days, was notorious for its two adjacent level crossings on the Parkstone side. There was a mile-long tramway through the streets to Poole Quay, closed in 1960, that had been the haunt of one or two Class B4 0-4-0Ts and there were extensive sidings for freight and empty carriage stock on the inside of the curving main line. No more than a mile from the station was Holes Bay Junction, where the direct spur to Hamworthy Junction came into use on 1 June 1893, curving away from the 1872 route to Broadstone Junction. At Hamworthy Junction there remains open the short branch to the original Poole terminus, despite it being reduced to freight only status almost a century ago; it was originally opened in 1847. Thence to Dorchester the line follows the western extremity of the 'Corkscrew', mostly through low-lying terrain as far as Wareham.

A 10-mile long branch to Corfe Castle and Swanage left the main line at Worgret Junction, being constructed after the usual local pressure and opened in 1885. Initially worked by Beattie 2-4-0WT locomotives, similar to those that survived in North Cornwall until 1962, the single track to Swanage saw the use of Bulleid Pacifics on summer through services after Nationalisation. Local trains were formed of the familiar push-pull set and 'M7' tank for many years — in fact, the Wareham-Swanage service was one of the last to be operated by motor-trains on the Southern, the engines being shedded at Bournemouth and used turn and turn about with those on the Brockenhurst and Lymington duties. Thereafter, until the end of steam, modern 2-6-2T and 2-6-4T designs were employed but these had to run round the carriages at both Wareham and Swanage. Freight traffic brought traditional 0-6-0s to

Below:
Dwarfed by the quayside cranes and one of the railway-owned ships, outside-cylinder pannier tank No 1369 waits until all passengers have boarded the Up Channel Islands boat train at Weymouth Quay on 28 April 1962 before departing through the streets to the main station.

the line until they, in turn, were displaced by the more versatile modern Standard 2-6-0s. However, following withdrawal of the passenger facilities at the beginning of 1972, it was traditional clay traffic from the Furzebrook area and oil deposits that kept a physical link open at Worgret: elsewhere track was lifted but this has now been progressively relaid northwards from Swanage as part of a preservation scheme. The intention is eventually to reconnect the branch to the main network.

At Dorchester there are two stations, relics of the day when rival railways served the county town. The Southampton & Dorchester Railway opened in 1847, having constructed a terminal at what is now the South station. Ten years later the Wilts, Somerset & Weymouth Railway (by then owned by the Great Western), extended southwards from Yeovil (Pen Mill), serving what is now Dorchester West. Agreement was reached between the LSWR and GWR for the former to have access from Dorchester Junction — just south of both stations — to Weymouth, so mixed gauge track had to be laid for the purpose. This worked in favour of the LSWR, for traffic routed over its standard gauge line avoided transhipment to or from the GWR's broad gauge; in the end the GWR bowed to the inevitable, converting the Weymouth line to standard gauge in 1874.

Formerly two branch lines connected with the Yeovil-Dorchester West-Weymouth line: the Abbotsbury branch diverged at Upwey Junction, on the joint section south of Dorchester, while that to Bridport (and, later, West Bay) went off at Maiden Newton, north of Dorchester. The Maiden Newton-Bridport branch was constructed first in 1857, to broad gauge standards, while the Abbotsbury line was not built until 1885; the extension from Bridport to West Bay opened in 1884. While West Bay lost its passenger services in 1930, all these lines survived to come into BR ownership upon Nationalisation in 1948. However, the Abbotsbury branch was an early casualty, closing to all traffic beyond Upwey from the end of November 1952. Goods trains to West Bay petered out in 1960, but because only minor roads served the rural country between Maiden Newton and Bridport, passenger traffic remained quite buoyant and outlived the end of steam. A rare feature of Maiden Newton was its inclined siding, which enabled locomotives to run round their train, as there was no loop provided clear of the main line. Regular steam-hauled passenger trains ceased in 1959, being replaced by through diesel services from Weymouth.

Most services to Abbotsbury were auto-trains, consisting of a little '14xx' 0-4-2T and trailer. When this was not required, for example on Sundays, it could be used to provide a through service from Weymouth to Maiden Newton and Bridport. On weekdays the Bridport branch train normally comprised a Pannier tank or small Prairie and two carriages. In the early years of Nationalisation, a GWR diesel railcar was tried on some local services between Yeovil and Weymouth, but it did not become a regular feature of operations. For the more important services to or from Weymouth various types of 4-6-0 were available: 'Halls' and 'Granges' were to be seen alongside the Hawksworth 'Counties' on mixed-traffic work, while 'Castles' tended to be reserved for the best trains. As for Southern services through to Weymouth, Bulleid Pacifics and 'King Arthur' 4-6-0s seemed to be favourites until the 'Standard' invasion.

Around Weymouth itself there were two more lines of special interest. Whilst the branch to Portland and Easton — a joint operation by the LSWR and GWR opened in two stages (to Portland in 1865 and to Easton in 1900) — lost its passenger services in 1952, freight continued until April 1965. Trains ran along the eastern extremity of the famous Chesil Beach to reach Portland, thence curving round in a great arc towards Easton, clinging to the cliffs and climbing all the while, the steepest gradient being 1 in 40! The other line was the Quay Tramway, which was worked by horses for some years after opening in 1865. Once locomotives came into use the possibility of expanding activities from purely freight loomed; after the Weymouth & Channel Islands Steam Packet's vessels had been acquired by the GWR in 1889, passenger trains ran on to the pier to connect with sailings. Because of the nature of the Tramway, running along the public highway for much of its route and with severe curvature in places, special locomotives were needed to operate it: as late as 1934 the GWR designed a class of six outside-cylinder Pannier tanks with Weymouth Quay in mind, three being the normal allocation to Weymouth in BR days. Nos 1367, 1368 and 1370 were the regular locomotives throughout the 1950s, but then No 1369 appeared in 1960 and, fresh from overhaul, returned to Quay duties in 1962 before transfer to North Cornwall later that same year. Drewry 204hp diesel shunters took over, but larger Panniers and the ex-LMS Class 2 2-6-2Ts made occasional forays through the streets until practically the final days of steam. The '1366' class Panniers allocated to Weymouth shed (initially coded 82F, later 71G) were fitted with a bell to supplement the usual whistle as a warning when working on the Tramway.

Weymouth shed was one of the last to operate steam locomotives in the south of England, engines being based and serviced there until the elimination of this evocative form of motive power in July 1967. Though their appearance, latterly, was generally shabby and unkempt, seldom was there any doubt of their capability to undertake the tasks they were required to do. Some of the pho-

tographs, taken in the last months of steam haulage, illustrate the sort of do-or-die philosophy that brought enthusiasts from all over Britain to record exploits that many feared would have to last a lifetime. This book is intended as a memorial to, and celebration of, steam at work in the counties of Hampshire and Dorset right to the end of the line.

Below:
Reminiscent of the time when railways carried the bulk of the nation's freight, Class 1366 0-6-0PT No 1370 shuffled through the back streets of Weymouth with fitted vans for the Channel Islands' traffic. As this was 31 May 1950, doubtless they would have been loaded at the quay with all manner of summer flowers and vegetables for London and other big cities, such traffic travelling overnight to reach its destination fresh. *J. C. Flemons*

Right:
Normal passenger services from Weymouth (Melcombe Regis) to Portland and Easton were suspended from March 1952, so it was a rare chance to see an enthusiasts' special travel over the branch on 14 August 1960. Ex-GWR 0-6-0PT No 3737 was recorded climbing away from Portland.

Right:
With the Isle of Portland looming in the background, a special train visiting the branch to Easton was returning to Weymouth (Melcombe Regis) on 27 March 1965. Provided with an engine at each end of the six carriages to avoid the need to run round, Class 2 2-6-2T No 41284 was bowling along the embankment by the eastern end of the famous Chesil Beach with No 41324 bringing up the rear.
M. Thresh

Right:
A glimpse of one of the traditional industries of the Isle of Portland, with Pannier tank No 9620 shunting stone wagons at Quarry Tip siding, Easton, in June 1958. The Portland branch closed to all traffic in 1965. *J. H. Lucking*

Left:
The branch to Abbotsbury closed in 1952, Upwey Junction being renamed Upwey & Broadwey station as a result. On 6 September 1966 Standard Class 4 2-6-0 No 76061 eased the 4.47pm Weymouth-Bournemouth Central local service to a stop at the former island platform. It was from the other side of this platform that the Abbotsbury branch descended steeply to Upwey station and goods yard; despite abandonment of all services over the rest of the line, freight facilities were retained at Upwey until the end of 1961. *J. Scrace*

Left:
With power shut off, Class H15 4-6-0 No 30475 drifts past the shed yard (71G) into Weymouth with the 12.53pm from Bournemouth Central on 19 June 1959. The rolling stock appears to have been marshalled oddly, for the second carriage is a non-corridor vehicle wedged between normal corridor coaches! An Up WR service is on the adjacent track. *K. L. Cook*

Left:
Something of the timeless fascination of steam can be appreciated from this study of a grimy pair of engines battling with the relentless 1 in 50 ascent north of Upwey & Broadwey in July 1966. A Standard 4-6-0 pilots a rebuilt 'West Country' with an 11-coach load from Weymouth to Waterloo, their combined exhaust creating shadows in the afternoon sunlight. *D. E. Canning*

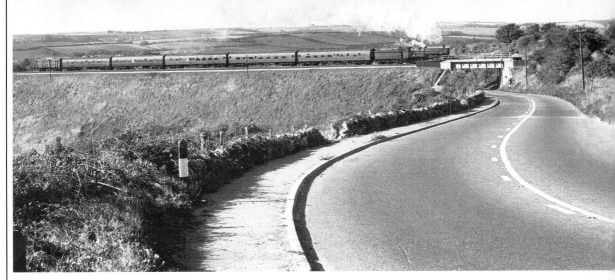

Above:
Struggling with the 1 in 50/52 that persisted as far as the Bincombe tunnels, past Upwey Wishing Well Halt, 4-6-0 No 7914 *Lleweni Hall* plods on with a morning special from Weymouth conveying flowers from the Channel Islands for mainland markets on 21 September 1964. *D. H. Cape*

Below:
On one of those crisp winter days that herald the approach of spring, Standard Class 5 4-6-0 No 73037 grinds up the steep gradient towards Upwey Wishing Well Halt with the 2.11pm Weymouth-Waterloo service on 27 February 1966. *Brian Stephenson*

Left:
Like a model railway at an exhibition, an immaculate rebuilt Bulleid Pacific — in this instance No 34042 *Dorchester* — emerges into the afternoon sunshine between the two Bincombe tunnels at the head of a train for Weymouth on 3 September 1964. *R. H. Tunstall*

Centre left:
In the deep cutting between the two Bincombe tunnels, 4-6-0 No 1027 *County of Stafford* wears Class 'A' headlamps appropriate for a Bristol (Temple Meads)-Weymouth service on 23 July 1960. The combination of squat double-chimney and two cylinders made the modern 'County' class somewhat untypical of the Swindon regime; not one survived into preservation. *Derek Cross*

Below left:
After all the effort of climbing up from Dorchester, 'West Country' 4-6-2 No 34093 *Saunton* has the regulator eased for the downhill run into Weymouth with an express from London (Waterloo); this train was recorded between the two Bincombe tunnels on 23 July 1960. *Derek Cross*

Right:
From their first exploits at the turn of the century to their demise 60 years later, Dugald Drummond's 'T9' 4-4-0s were associated particularly with the West Country. On 14 August 1960 one of the last survivors, No 30718, was selected to work a special from Salisbury to Weymouth via Yeovil. After a taxing assault on the steep climb to Evershot, the old warrior had an easier time of it — with a scorched smokebox door, No 30718 ambled towards Dorchester West during one of the day's fine intervals.

Left:
Framed in the entrance to the goods depot, 0-6-0PT No 4689 bustles out of Maiden Newton with the 4.30pm local train to Weymouth on 16 May 1959. Though the bracket signal in the picture is a typical GW/WR product, other signals at the station owe more allegiance to Waterloo than to Paddington thanks to post-Nationalisation boundary changes.

Below:
Maiden Newton was the junction for the Bridport branch. Standard Class 5 4-6-0 No 73018 leaves the station with a clean exhaust when heading through coaches from Weymouth to Paddington; on the right, the Bridport 'B' set stands on the inclined siding held by handbrake. Meanwhile, 0-6-0PT No 3737 stands in the bay platform awaiting the signal to come out on to the branch, to enable the 'B' set to be released to run back into the station by gravity, thus allowing the tank engine to resume its proper place for the next service to Bridport. The date is 16 May 1959.

Right:
The 5.15pm branch train from Maiden Newton to Bridport stops at Toller station on 16 May 1959, nestling amid the rolling Dorset countryside made famous by Thomas Hardy in his novels — here, if anywhere, one could believe in *Far from the Madding Crowd*. While BR closed the little railway in 1975, Toller station has been painstakingly rebuilt as Littlehempston Riverside at Totnes in Devon.

Right:
In pouring rain, Gresley Class A3 4-6-2 No 60112 *St Simon* stormed through Wareham station on 25 August 1963 at the head of the 'Southern Counties Enterprise' special bound for Weymouth. Numerically the last of the class, it is believed this was the only appearance on the Southern Region of this particular locomotive; *Flying Scotsman* (formerly No 60103) hauled one or two specials after preservation and overhaul in 1966. *W. G. Sumner*

Right:
Following withdrawal of the 'M7s', branch services to Swanage became the province of 2-6-2T locomotives. On 10 June 1964 Class 2 No 41312 was at Wareham with the 11.10am for Swanage formed of a converted Maunsell push-pull set. None of the replacement locomotives was equipped with compatible control gear, so push-pull trains became a thing of the past. *J. Scrace*

Above:
From the steep slope below the ruins of Corfe Castle, Ivatt Class 2 2-6-2T No 41224 was spotted working the 2.35pm Swanage-Wareham service bunker-first on 16 October 1965, passing a small car travelling in the opposite direction on the road below. *M. J. Fox*

Above right:
Watched by a throng of admirers, Standard Class 4 2-6-0 No 76026 prepares to leave Corfe Castle for Wareham following the visit of a special train to the Swanage branch on 7 May 1967. On this date steam took over the entire branch, running several journeys with different motive power for the benefit of enthusiasts and photographers.

Below right:
Deputising for a push-pull 'M7', Standard Class 3 2-6-2T No 82029 strides along the low embankment between Worgret Junction and Furzebrook with a Wareham-Swanage branch train one chill March day in 1964. Not especially favoured among Western Region crews (who preferred their traditional Swindon Prairies), the Standard Class 3s were, however, popular on the Southern for both passenger and freight duties.

Left:
Recalling times past when Swanage was served by through services from Waterloo, which might bring Bulleid Light Pacific locomotives on to the branch, 'West Country' 4-6-2 No 34023 *Blackmore Vale* had a full head of steam as it departed from Corfe Castle for the terminus on 7 May 1967.

Left:
Coasting into Swanage past the signal cabin and stone goods shed, Standard Class 4 2-6-0 No 76011 arrives at the terminus with the 12.23pm branch service from Wareham on 10 July 1966. Services were progressively run down until withdrawal of all passenger traffic in January 1972, but, after an uphill struggle, a preservation society has succeeded in reopening part of the single-line route as a tourist attraction.
Ian Allan Library

Left:
The 'Hampshire Venturer' special leaves Holes Bay Junction behind as it makes for Hamworthy Junction as part of its tour of lines around Poole Harbour. After running round, the 'Q' class 0-6-0 tender engine (No 30548) will take the train chimney-first via Upton and Broadstone Junction before returning via Ringwood to London. The route from Hamworthy to Ringwood and beyond was to follow exactly the course of the Southampton & Dorchester Railway opened in 1847.
R. A. Panting

Preservation

Above:
Following closure of the line from Alton to Winchester a preservation group was established initially to take over the whole route. These plans proved over optimistic and services were limited originally to the Alresford-Ropley section. Subsequently, the line has been relaid between Ropley and Alton, where a connection is made with British Rail. Here Nos 31874 and 506 haul an excursion from British Rail past Ropley on 3 October 1987. *John H. Bird*

Below:
Although part of the Swanage branch survived to serve freight trains to Furzebrook, the remainder was lifted after closure. The trackbed, however, survived and is now being relaid by the preservation society. With the repatriated 'M7' in the platform at Swanage it is possible to imagine the scene as it was 30 years ago. In reality the date was 9 April 1987. *Michael H. C. Baker*

Above:
Tailpiece
On a bright autumn day an Up express wails a warning as it thunders through Sherborne station on the erstwhile Southern main line to the west. Headed by an immaculate 'Merchant Navy' Pacific, No 35028 *Clan Line*, the headboard reads 'Blackmore Vale Express'. The well-filled train is returning from Yeovil Junction to Salisbury and the date is 4 October 1986! Can there be a more poignant celebration of steam than its triumphal home-coming after two decades of banishment?